PRAISE FOR *ST[...]* INTERRUPTED FORMAL EDUCATION

"Students with limited or interrupted formal education are a growing population in our schools and one that few of our teachers are prepared to serve well. Their social and educational needs are often quite different from those of the majority of culturally and linguistically diverse students and other English as an additional language learners. This book has many resources and suggestions for assistance with serving the needs of these students. Additionally I am glad to see the book addresses resiliency and culture shock, as these are two areas frequently overlooked in textbooks for teachers working with these challenging students."

—Catherine Collier, PhD, Director
CrossCultural Developmental Education Services
Ferndale, WA

"With *Students With Interrupted Formal Education: Bridging Where They Are and What They Need,* Custodio and O'Loughlin have produced an important resource for teachers, school leaders, teacher educators, and community leaders. The authors show readers the many challenges that students with interrupted formal education (SIFE) face and provide critical background information on these English learners. Then the authors give specific strategies for supporting these students academically, socially, and culturally. They include checklists, application ideas, and bibliographies. This book is a must-read for all those working with SIFEs."

—Yvonne Freeman, Professor Emerita
The University of Texas at Brownsville
Brownsville, TX

"In a much-needed new resource, Brenda Custodio and Judith O'Loughlin address a unique subgroup of English learners with empathy, aptitude, and critical insight. *Students With Interrupted Formal Education: Bridging Where They Are and What They Need* provides a comprehensive picture of the complex context and rich diversity among SIFEs, while it also offers field-tested, ready-to-use, specific suggestions on how to create a positive support system for SIFEs that lead to student success! I am excited to see the well-deserved attention the authors have given to this hard-to-reach and sometimes underserved group of students."

—Andrea Honigsfeld, PhD, Associate Dean and EdD, Program Director
Molloy College
Rockville Centre, NY

"Custodio and O'Loughlin provide a thorough yet focused discussion of SIFE and what teachers can do to support them. Their text is recommended for those who work with these students and for those who prepare them to do so."

—Timothy A. Micek, DA, Associate Professor and Director
Ohio Dominican University and MATESOL
Columbus, OH

"Finally, we have an insightful and timely comprehensive resource for our schools that will be immensely helpful to serving the growing numbers of refugee and immigrant children in our classrooms today! So many of these children have fled severe persecution, war, and poverty, which means months or even years of missed schooling. With a deeply compassionate perspective based on their years of rich experience and research, Custodio and O'Loughlin cover it all in this book. Both vulnerable and resilient, these children have shown how successful they can be when classrooms are welcoming and build on their strengths. This practical book will provide educators—and all those who care about these children—with just the information and resources they need. Bravo to Custodio and O'Loughlin—they have produced the first book of its kind that will be critical to the success of these children and our increasingly global education system!"

—Lyn Morland, MSW, MA, Research Fellow
Bank Street College of Education, Center for
Culturally Responsive Practice
New York, NY

"This seminal work is the fruit of extensive research and many years of classroom experience on the part of the authors, who truly represent the vanguard in working with students with interrupted formal education. With clarity and precision, it offers practical steps that teachers, other educational professionals, and districts at large can take to champion these students to academic and social success. Designed with great compassion for an increasingly significant student population, it is indispensable for both seasoned and younger educators alike. Especially in light of today's political climate, it outlines extensive and highly innovative strategies that draw upon students' previous knowledge and background to reveal what is essential for their education and acculturation."

—Bruce Williams, PhD, Graduate Director,
Bilingual Education and ESL
William Paterson University, Department
of Languages and Cultures
Wayne, NJ

*I dedicate this book to Columbus (OH)
City Schools and The Ohio State University.
Together they have shaped my professional
and academic life.*

—Brenda Custodio

*I dedicate this book to my husband, Joseph, and
my daughters, Jennifer Petraglia and Amy Morse,
for all their support and encouragement in
every endeavor I undertake.*

*I also dedicate this book to my Aunt Carrie Testa
(1923–2016) who reminded me often that life was
an adventure, no matter what the obstacles,
detours, and wrong turns I might take.*

—Judith O'Loughlin

STUDENTS WITH INTERRUPTED FORMAL EDUCATION

BRIDGING WHERE THEY ARE AND WHAT THEY NEED

BRENDA CUSTODIO
JUDITH B. O'LOUGHLIN

Foreword by Deborah Short

CORWIN
A SAGE Publishing Company

FOR INFORMATION:

Corwin

A SAGE Company

2455 Teller Road

Thousand Oaks, California 91320

(800) 233-9936

www.corwin.com

SAGE Publications Ltd.

1 Oliver's Yard

55 City Road

London EC1Y 1SP

United Kingdom

SAGE Publications India Pvt. Ltd.

B 1/I 1 Mohan Cooperative Industrial Area

Mathura Road, New Delhi 110 044

India

SAGE Publications Asia-Pacific Pte. Ltd.

3 Church Street

#10-04 Samsung Hub

Singapore 049483

Program Director: Dan Alpert

Senior Associate Editor: Kimberly Greenberg

Editorial Assistant: Katie Crilley

Production Editor: Amy Schroller

Copy Editor: Lana Todorovic-Arndt

Typesetter: C&M Digitals (P) Ltd.

Proofreader: Rae-Ann Goodwin

Cover Designer: Rose Storey

Marketing Manager: Maura Sullivan

Printed in the United States of America

Library of Congress Cataloging-in-Publication Data

Names: Custodio, Brenda, author. | O'Loughlin, Judith B., author.

Title: Students with interrupted formal education : bridging where they are and what they need / Brenda Custodio, Ohio State University (retired), Judith B. O'Loughlin.

Description: Thousand Oaks, California : Corwin, [2017] | Includes bibliographical references and index.

Identifiers: LCCN 2016055828 | ISBN 9781506359656 (pbk. : alk. paper)

Subjects: LCSH: Children of immigrants—Education—United States. | English language—Study and teaching—Foreign speakers.

Classification: LCC LC3746 .C87 2017 | DDC 371.826/9120973—dc23 LC record available at https://lccn.loc.gov/2016055828

This book is printed on acid-free paper.

17 18 19 20 21 10 9 8 7 6 5 4 3 2 1

CONTENTS

FOREWORD

We know that many English learners struggle in U.S. elementary and secondary schools because they are expected to learn academic English and subject area curricula at the same time. As English learners they are not yet proficient in English, but they are held to the same standards and accountability benchmarks as native English speakers with only some modest accommodations regarding how soon and in what manner they must take high-stakes assessments, which in most states are offered solely in English. The burden this situation places on the students, their teachers, and their schools is unfair; and test results are not valid indicators of student knowledge, but it is today's reality.

We also know that although English learners are often lumped together as one subgroup in the PK-12 school population, they have very diverse linguistic, cultural, and academic backgrounds. While over 70% of the English learners in our schools were born in the United States, others have come to our country as immigrants, refugees, and asylees. Many have come with family members and some have been unaccompanied. Some have had smooth journeys and others, traumatic ones. Some have left behind happy memories and others, turmoil and despair. Most however arrive with the hope for a better future. Among the new arrivals are the learners this book focuses on, Students with Interrupted Formal Education, or SIFE. They are a small subset of all the English learners but they are particularly vulnerable and their success in school is not guaranteed. They have the farthest to go to catch up to their English-speaking peers. And when they enter our schools and programs at middle and high school, they face significant social and academic challenges and a limited period of time to master all the content needed for graduation and become proficient in academic English.

In some school districts these students enter specially designed newcomer programs that can ease their integration and build background knowledge for school courses, but in others they are placed in regular ESL or bilingual classrooms where the curricula may not be suited to their needs (DeCapua, Smathers & Tang, 2009; Short & Boyson, 2012). These students have not had schooling on par with their age-level peers. They may have missed a few years because of war, geography, or the inability to pay school fees, or they may have never attended school because they lived in a refugee camp. Some may have literacy in their native language, but many do not. Yet, the gaps in their education do not reflect a lack of intelligence or motivation to learn, just the lack of opportunity. In fact, these students by many reports are among the most eager to be studying in school.

One of the guiding principles of effective English language teaching is for educators to know their students. To best educate students with interrupted formal education, we need to know their backgrounds and interests, and understand their needs. These needs go far beyond English literacy development and other academic goals.

And that in a nutshell captures the value of this book. Besides discussing academic strategies and program supports, Custodio and O'Loughlin familiarize educators to the sociocultural and socioemotional needs of SIFE. They provide key background information on these students' languages and cultures, and in some cases conflicts that have occurred in their home countries. They describe in rich detail some of the personal challenges (such as dealing with trauma experienced in their home country or getting along with a parent not seen in 10 years) and family challenges (such as finding housing and jobs) that these learners face. In addition, they suggest steps that teachers and other school staff can take to create a climate that welcomes the students and alleviates some of their concerns while also giving them resources to adjust socially and thrive academically.

In Chapter 1, educators can learn about the diversity among SIFE and consider the type of information that schools should collect upon their enrollment to learn the students' backgrounds, educational gaps, and knowledge they bring to school more fully. Chapter 2 describes important factors in immigrant youth's home countries and educational systems that have bearing on their families' expectations for schooling and life in the United States. The push and pull of immigration is discussed as are the uncertainties and limited opportunities some of the families confront in the United States. The focus of Chapter 3 is on refugees and the resettlement process. Particularly useful are the descriptions of some of the more frequently resettled groups, and what strengths they have that educators can develop further and what challenges they face that educators should prepare for.

The second half of the book, Chapters 4 and 5, helps educators pull together what they have learned about their students to create programs that address their sociocultural, socioemotional, and academic needs. Practical tools are included here, such as strategies to strengthen student resiliency, checklists for guiding teacher behaviors in class and for establishing a positive school climate, lists of books and guidelines for selecting others that are appropriate for SIFE, a sample standards-based lesson plan, and a student observation form to help measure performance. Recommendations for programming are explained, from newcomer and expanded learning programs to sheltered instruction classes and assistance with postsecondary options. Nonacademic supports, such as wraparound services for families and connections to the community networks, are also explored.

This book, *Students With Interrupted Formal Education: Bridging Where They Are and What They Need*, offers a "whole child" approach to serving this at-risk student population. English learners, and SIFE especially, are often defined by what they lack, be it English proficiency, subject area knowledge, or cultural competence. The compassion that Custodio and O'Loughlin feel for these students, the commitment they have to educating them well, and the comprehension they have of the assets these learners bring to the classroom is evident in the writing, tools, and vignettes they share.

As Gándara (2015) has noted, strengths of English learners include knowledge of the native language (they are emerging bilinguals), resiliency, problem-solving skills, collaborative learning styles, the ability to consider different perspectives, and motivation. This book acknowledges these qualities and will help educators build on them. Use the book to generate productive conversations in professional learning communities and study groups to better understand your students and give them the best educational, socioemotional, and sociocultural supports possible. Help ensure the promise of a better future for them.

—Deborah Short

PREFACE

This book has been several years in creation. As we, the authors, have worked with the educators of English learners across the country, we continue to see a rise in the number of students who are entering our classrooms with significant gaps in their academic knowledge. For many of these students, the main cause of these gaps is the limited formal education they experienced in their home country. We will examine the situations that created this interrupted education and give suggestions for helping students find internal and external supports that will help bridge those gaps and lead to academic success.

Before you begin reading, we want to state up front that we are basing this book on certain critical underlying assumptions. The first and foremost of these assumptions is that these students can learn and progress, often at an alarming speed. But they will need time, attention, and a specific focus. They have unique needs that may not be met in the typical ESL or bilingual classroom, and certainly cannot be met in the typical mainstream classroom without intensive support when they first arrive. Those supports can be tapered off as the student begins to close in on his or her peers, but they cannot be ignored.

Second, we believe that culture counts with all students, and that a certain level of knowledge of the history and background of each student is important. It helps us as adults build empathy for the experiences and perspective of the students in our classrooms. We do not have to be experts on each language and culture, but we do need a basic understanding of the political, religious, and cultural backgrounds of our students.

We also strongly believe that we teach a whole child and that education is not limited to academic knowledge alone. We must meet the physical, emotional, and social needs of our students in order for them to be "ready to learn." A child who is sick, afraid, angry, or hungry is not going to be able to concentrate. It is our responsibility as human beings to take care of all our children.

ACKNOWLEDGMENTS

Writing this book has been a wonderful and collaborative experience for both of us, from the first time we sat down with Dan Alpert, Corwin Acquisitions Editor, at the TESOL Convention in Toronto and described our ideas for a book about students with interrupted formal education (SIFE). Dan listened, made suggestions, encouraged us, and helped us to believe that we could and should write this book. Dan made it obvious from the beginning that he believed in us and in the importance of this topic. In addition to Dan, we would also like to thank the Corwin team, especially Katie Crilley for her editorial suggestions and help through the production process, Maura Sullivan for her creative approach to cover design, and Lana Arndt and Amy Schroller for their tireless editing.

There are others we would like to thank who have helped us as we wrote. We'd like to thank Barbara Page, who worked in the Saturday Newcomer Academy in Beaverton, and Mary Lou McCloskey with the Global Village Project for sharing information on amazing programs that support English learners outside the typical school day. Thanks to Luis F. Macias, Sonia Colon, and Jose Luis Morales Crispin who shared their perspective on Latino education issues. Thank you to the lawyers at Advocates for Basic Legal Equality for their tireless efforts to support unaccompanied minors.

We want to express a very special thank you to all the resettlement workers in the United States and Canada who give of their time and talents to ease the transition for our refugee families. Additionally, we would like to thank Lehrhaus Judaica, San Francisco, (www.lehrhaus .org/about/) for providing education programs to inform the public and encourage community members to help refugees in their community. We admire Jewish Family and Community Services, East Bay (www.jfcs-eastbay.org), for their work encouraging volunteers to perform a variety of services for families, or to start and continue collection drives for resources needed by refugee families, as well a working toward finding safe homes for refugees in the Bay Area of San Francisco.

We want to acknowledge all the participants in our various sessions across the country who have told us their stories and shared their experiences with us. They inspired us to continue writing and advocating for newcomers and students with interrupted education.

Both of us would like to acknowledge the role that TESOL, Inc. has played in both of our professional lives, including the affiliates, NJTESOL-NJBE, CATESOL (California), and Ohio TESOL, in which we have been active as members and taken on leadership roles. We thank and admire John Segota, TESOL Associate Executive Director for Public Policy and Professional Relations, because he has taught us how to advocate for English learners at the local, state, and national levels. We have been inspired to advocate for SIFE English learners through the annual TESOL Advocacy and Policy sessions and speakers.

We especially want to thank Dr. Deborah Short for the role she has played in shining a spotlight on newcomers across the country, as well as for her willingness to write the foreword for this book.

We also want to acknowledge those educators listed below who took their valuable time to read and review this book. They helped shape and validate our work.

Finally, I (Judith O'Loughlin) would like to thank and acknowledge Dr. Keumsil Kim Yoon and Dr. Bruce Williams at William Paterson University, Languages and Cultures Department for providing me with a Title VII Teacher Training Grant, which was the start of my journey as a teacher and advocate for English learners, newcomers, but especially for SIFE students.

Publisher's Acknowledgments

Corwin gratefully acknowledges the contributions of the following reviewers:

Suzanne M. Carey
Special Education Teacher
Perth Amboy High School
Amboy, NJ

Brian E. Fernandes
Reading Specialist/Literacy Coach and Mentor
Hampden Meadows School
Barrington, RI

Dr. Marian K. Hermie
Retired Superintendent and Adjunct Faculty
Grand Canyon University
Phoenix, AZ

Ken Klopack
Art and Gifted Education Consultant
Chicago Public Schools
Chicago, IL

Karen Kozy-Landress
Pre-K Support Specialist
Brevard Public Schools
Titusville, FL

James L. Morrison
Educator and Financial Analyst
University of Oklahoma, College of Liberal Studies
Norman, OK

Chantal Normil, Ed.D.
Director of ESOL
Clayton County Public Schools
Jonesboro, GA

Olivia Elizondo Zepeda
Associate Superintendent
Gadsden Elementary School District #32
San Luis, AZ

ABOUT THE AUTHORS

 **Brenda Custodio** is retired from Columbus City Schools (Ohio) where she served as a middle and high school ESL teacher, a district-level coach for secondary ESL teachers, and a building administrator of a newcomer secondary academy. She worked with the school district to help establish a newcomer program for middle and high school students with a large refugee population, most of whom had limited prior schooling.

Dr. Custodio developed the program for use by Ohio State University to train alternative license candidates through a federal grant and served as a coach for several years for the teachers enrolled in the program. She has served as an educational consultant for several school districts in Ohio and has worked as a teacher trainer for the Ohio Department of Education on the topics of refugee education and unaccompanied minors. She has developed curriculum and programming for both high school and adult refugee students with limited home language literacy.

Her professional responsibilities have included president and conference chair of Ohio TESOL, chair of the Secondary Schools Interest Section and the Refugee Concerns Interest Section of TESOL, Inc., and membership on the international Professional Development Committee. She has been awarded the Winston Churchill Traveling Fellowship Grant to visit Australia, the Moira McKenzie Literacy Grant to work with Dr. Gay Su Pennell, and is a five-time recipient of the Ameritech Impact II Grant. She received the Ohio TESOL Outstanding Achievement Award twice, and also the 2016 Lifetime Achievement Award by the same organization.

Dr. Custodio is currently preparing preservice and inservice teachers at the Ohio State University to work in second-language classrooms. As a frequent presenter at both the state and national level, she has presented on the topics of literacy development for adolescents, unique needs of refugee students, culturally diverse classrooms, newcomer programming, and students with interrupted formal education. Her first book on the topic of Newcomers has led to site visits in Massachusetts, New York, New Jersey, Virginia, Maryland, Florida, Minnesota, Washington, California, Texas, Pennsylvania, Ohio, and Toronto, Ontario.

 **Judith B. O'Loughlin,** an independent education consultant, has 25 years of experience as an English, ESL, and special education teacher. She has taught ESL at K–12, adult education, and graduate levels in university endorsement programs in New Jersey, Missouri, Massachusetts, Kansas, and Ohio. She is currently a bilingual/ESL eCoach for preservice candidates for The Ohio State University "Transition to Teaching" grant.

While teaching in New Jersey, Judith worked as a consultant with the New Jersey Department of Education, Office of Bilingual/ESL Education on standards and assessment for English learners, developed a draft of ESL/ELA Standards, low-incidence ESL programming and instruction, and provided inservice sessions throughout the state about sheltered instruction for English learners in mainstream classrooms.

As an independent consultant, Judith focuses on standards-based curriculum, instructional strategies, differentiated instruction, addressing the needs of newcomers, formative assessment, and collegial collaboration for ESL and mainstream co-teaching. Recently, Judith was an invited presenter at the 2014 TESOL Academy in Columbus Ohio, June 20–21, 2014, and Stockton University, New Jersey, on June 19–20, 2015. For the latter program, she worked with 25 visiting linguistic professors from Pakistan. Her topic focused on ELL Writing and Formative Assessment. She is a certified WIDA Consultant in Standards and Assessment, as well as a Pearson SIOP Certified Trainer.

Ms. O'Loughlin previously served on the NJTESOL-NJBE Executive Board as president, and currently serves on both the CATESOL Board of Directors as Conference Services Coordinator and Advocacy, as well as the CATESOL Education Foundation vice president. She is also the 2015–2017 chair of the TESOL Standards Professional Council.

Ms. O'Loughlin was the 2015 CATESOL Sadae Iwataki Service Award recipient and one of the TESOL "50 at 50" recognized leaders in the field, as nominated by her peers. She has previously received the 2003 Seton Hall University, Multicultural Education Teacher of the Year and the 2001 NJTESOL-NJBE Leadership Award.

INTRODUCTION TO STUDENTS WITH INTERRUPTED FORMAL EDUCATION

STUDENTS WITH INTERRUPTED FORMAL EDUCATION (SIFE): DEFINITION AND BACKGROUND

Students with interrupted formal education, also known by the acronym SIFE, are a relatively small proportion of recently arrived English learners, probably somewhere between 10% and 20% (Advocates for Children of New York, 2010; Ruiz-de-Velasco & Fix, 2000). However, these students often represent the neediest of our English learners because of their limited first-language literacy, frequent gaps in academic knowledge and skills, and sometimes, critical social and emotional needs.

As discussed in the preface, it is the belief of the authors that educators and other professionals who have the responsibility and the privilege of getting to know these students, and who will be helping them to reach their full potential, need to have an understanding of where these students have been and why they may have certain gaps in their academic knowledge. This knowledge will build empathy for the students. It can also help classroom teachers discover the most effective methodologies and materials that will bridge the gap between what SIFE already know and can do, and what they will be expected to be able to do in their new academic setting. Since most English learners (ELs) spend the majority of their school day in mainstream classrooms, we hope that all teachers will see the value in knowing more about the background of their students and how their previous educational experiences (or lack thereof!) impact their ability to perform on a daily basis.

So, who are these students, and where are they coming from?

> These students come from all over the world—from countries experiencing war, conflict, or environmental catastrophes. They come from refugee camps and isolated rural communities and many have been in transit for a number of years. In all these circumstances, their formal education has been limited, interrupted or even non-existent. (*English Literacy Development*, 2014, p. 1)

The highest percentage of SIFE in the United States are coming from Latin America, mainly Mexico, Central America, and the Caribbean. Refugee children make up the second highest number, with students from Asia, Africa, and the Middle East. Other smaller groups are composed of immigrant children from countries where schools were poorly equipped, teachers inadequately trained, or where school was not accessible due to geography, economics, or religion.

> Students who have these characteristics [of being SIFE] could be refugees, migrant students, or any student who experienced limited or interrupted access to school for a variety of reason, such as poverty, isolated geographic locales, limited transportation options, societal expectations for school attendance, a need to enter the workforce and contribute to the family income, natural disasters, war, or civil strife. (*Focus on SLIFE*, 2015, p. 1)

Chapter 2 will explain in detail the issues that are pushing students out of several Latin American countries and pulling them to the United States. Some are coming for economic reasons and others to join family members already living here. Some had strong educational experiences before beginning the trek north; others had experienced sporadic schooling in poorly equipped facilities. Most have gaps in their schooling because of the rigors of the journey and the length of the trip.

Chapter 3 will look at refugees and the challenges they face entering schools in the United States and Canada. As schools ramp up the expectations for students with higher academic standards, mandated assessments, and tougher college entrance exams; refugee students are often coming with the most rudimentary of skills. After years of war, **trauma**, and life in a camp, adjusting to rigorous secondary coursework requiring high levels of academic English can be overwhelming. Suggestions for assisting these students will be given in the second half of this book.

CHARACTERISTICS OF SIFE

What specifically defines these students and sets them apart from a "typical" English learner? David and Yvonne Freeman (2002, p. 33) created this list to describe a student with limited formal schooling. They stated that these students

- are overage for their grade-level placement due to their weak academic skills and limited or inadequate formal schooling,
- have needs that traditional ESL [English as a second language] and bilingual programs, and regular ESL programs, can't or don't meet,
- have low or sometimes even no literacy skills in their first language and/or in English, and have little academic content-area knowledge,
- are socially and psychologically isolated from mainstream students,
- need approaches and materials that will help them catch up to and compete with mainstream students, and
- are at risk of failing or dropping out in traditional academic programs.

The final bullet point, the higher dropout rate of SIFE students, is especially disturbing. Richard Fry, of the Pew Research Center, estimates that about 70% of the recent immigrants with interrupted schooling drop out of high school (Fry, 2005)! Why are we seeing this huge number? One strong possibility is that the support these students are currently receiving is not adequate to meet their needs.

> While recent arrivals who had schooling difficulties before migration clearly have elevated dropout rates, are there enough of them to make much of a difference? In the aggregate, the answer is clearly yes. For most countries of origin, there are enough of these youths and their dropout rates are high enough that they constitute a significant portion of the dropouts from that country. More than half of the dropouts from Guatemala are recent arrivals who had schooling difficulties before migrating. And 10 percent of the dropouts from the Caribbean (other than Puerto Rico) are recent arrivals with interrupted schooling abroad. The importance of recent arrivals with relatively low schooling upon arrival is pertinent to understanding the schooling difficulties of youths from countries of origin besides just Mexico and Central America. (Fry, 2005, p. 12)

In addition to the dropout rate associated with students with interrupted education, there is the strong possibility that many of these young people never bother to enroll in school at all. While this book will look at what educators can do to provide assistance and support for the students who enter our classrooms, a larger societal issue is the number of students who choose work over school.

> The dropout rate for teens with school problems before migration is in excess of 70 percent, in comparison with 8 percent for other foreign-born youths. And their characteristics, especially for males, suggest that many of them are labor migrants. Their purpose in migrating was probably to seek employment in the labor market, and they may have never enrolled in U.S. schools. Recently arrived males who did not make adequate school progress before migration are twice as likely to be working as other foreign-born males, and nearly 40 percent of them are in the agriculture and construction industries, in comparison with 10 percent of other foreign-born youths. In contrast to the living arrangements of other foreign-born youths, the majority of recent arrivals with prior school problems do not reside with any parent in the household. Given their participation in the labor market and the degree to which they were behind in school, the prospects of enrolling these youths in traditional high school settings appear to be remote. (Fry, 2005, p. 1)

What can be done to find and assist these adolescents is an issue beyond the parameters of this book, but it is a situation that needs to be addressed.

Chapters 4 and 5 will offer specific suggestions and recommendations for providing support systems for SIFE that will help them overcome the missing years of education and adjust to life in their new environment.

Unfortunately, the programming designed for ELs with academic skills and first language literacy, as well as for the students who have been in Western schools for most if not all of their education, is not sufficient for most students with interrupted schooling. The gap between what students are expected to be able to do and the skill set that students have at their disposal is often too great, and students frequently give up.

> Immigrant students with some academic skills are often able to make up the years they have lost to poverty or political strife in 2 or 3 years of concentrated coursework in content areas that is adapted to meet their language needs. In contrast, immigrant students lacking rudimentary literacy skills in their native language

are especially challenged in secondary school and may need many years of intensive work in order to graduate or make the transition to an appropriate program. (Mace-Matluck, Alexander-Kasparik, & Queen, 1998, p. 13)

Students with interrupted education need specialized programming and assistance, above and beyond what is normally provided to English language learners. This belief is supported in a recent **WIDA** statement about SIFE: "Students with this background [SIFE] often need their emotional, psychological, and physiological needs to be met before they are able to engage fully in the educational setting" (*Focus on SLIFE*, 2015, p. 2). The second half of this book will go into greater detail on how to help students build literacy in their home language and English, fill in the gap in content knowledge, and support the emotional and social needs of the student.

The Council of Chief State School Officers (*Immigrant Students and Secondary School Reform*, 2004, p. 11) created this list of supports they recommend for secondary newcomers (including those with interrupted education):

1. Build environments that respond to the immediate social, cultural, and linguistic needs of immigrant adolescents with limited schooling.

2. Create structures that transcend high school academic departmental divisions to support simultaneous linguistic and academic development.

3. Form newcomer centers to ease transitions for newly immigrated students.

4. Implement flexible scheduling to reflect real needs and obligations of high school immigrants.

5. Align high school programs with higher education and adult education.

6. Use the full resources of the community to support immigrant students.

IDENTIFICATION OF SIFE

One of the challenges of working with students with interrupted education is simply identification. Many school districts don't keep track of how much education students have received in their home country and their level of first-language literacy. Even when schools do ask, the answers are not always as helpful as it is assumed they would be. First of all, parents may state that their children have 6 or 8 years of schooling, but attendance may have been sporadic; they may have attended one-room schoolhouses with poorly trained teachers; or school may have only been for a few hours a day. Sometimes, the parents do not want to admit that their child was not in school regularly out of fear that they may not be permitted to enroll. They may not want to admit that the child was not able to attend because of the inability to pay for required books or uniforms, or that the child stayed home regularly to provide needed income for the family. In some countries, children with learning issues are not able to be provided for in a regular school setting, and the child simply stays home. To guarantee that their child will be admitted to the new school, certain facts are not disclosed, or the parents may not realize how schooling is different in their new setting.

> Gaps in school attendance are often due to sensitive matters; parents/guardians may be embarrassed, distressed, or feel threatened if they sense in any way they are being censured or blamed for the lack of complete [and accurate] school records or their children's incomplete prior educational experiences. (DeCapua, Smathers, & Tang, 2009, p. 10)

However, it is important that schools collect as much data as possible about each student and share that information with the classroom teacher. Providing the best instructional program for each child requires knowledge of previous literacy and content instruction. A sample data collection form is provided in Table 1.1 that can be adapted to the needs of the school/district.

PLACEMENT AND ENROLLMENT

The sample form in Table 1.1 contains suggested information to be collected upon enrollment to determine the type and level of previous education for each student. Obviously, the interviewer needs to speak the language of the family or have access to a translator that the family trusts. As much as possible, it is important to explain the reason for the questions; that the answers will be used to help provide the most appropriate schooling for the child; and that the answers will not determine if the child is permitted to enroll.

Table 1.1

Placement and Enrollment Information Form
What is your child's home country? _____
At what age did he or she leave the home country? _____
What is your child's home language? _____
Was this the language of instruction in his or her school? _____
If not, what was the language used in school in the home country? _____
Is your child literate in his or her first language? Yes / No
At what age did your child begin attending school? _____
How many years of education were completed in the home country? _____
What was the last year of schooling for your child? _____
Has your child studied English before arrival? Yes / No
For how many years? _____
Does you child have complete records from the home country? Yes / No
Has your child attended school in another school in the United States? Yes / No
Where and for how long? _____
Did you bring the records? Yes / No
Before coming to the United States, was your child separated from other family members? Yes / No
For how long? _____
Has your child ever lived in a refugee camp? Yes / No
Notes for placement:
Number of years behind peers in schooling (if applicable): _____
Records/transcripts from home country: Yes / No

Note for Schools: It is highly recommended that students be placed with children of the same age, even if the student has received little or no previous education. Placing a child back with younger children can have serious social and emotional consequences.

ELEMENTARY STUDENTS WITH INTERRUPTED EDUCATIONS

Although most programs for SIFE are developed for secondary students, elementary age students may have difficulty adjusting and meeting classroom demands as well. The challenges increase with the grade level, as the gap between what the student is capable of doing and the requirements of the classroom grows. This is true for all students with an interrupted education, but especially true for refugee children.

Having spent much of their childhood years in refugee camps, or even having been born into a refugee camp, elementary age newcomers may arrive with extremely limited or no formal schooling. Their daily experiences may not have included reading or writing activities in any language due to limited resources, including native language reading and writing materials. Without any formal education, elementary students would have little or no sound–symbol correspondence understanding before arriving in U.S. schools. They may never have held a pencil or scissors, used crayons, colored pencils or markers, handled **manipulatives** (e.g., dice, counters, etc.), or written on paper. They lack understanding of school repertoires, including sitting for extended periods of time at a desk or table, working cooperatively with classmates, eating in a lunchroom, using an American-style lavatory, and participating in conventional classroom, physical education, art, and music activities.

There are many school challenges for these newcomers. They will need to learn how to wait in line, take turns, stay in one place at a desk for long periods of time, and use school instruments (e.g., pencils, notebooks, textbooks, manipulatives, and technology). They will also be introduced to new foods and hygiene routines. Teachers will need to be patient, as processing new and unique information, understanding of patterns of behavior, and understanding school expectations will be learned very slowly. The overwhelming amount of input, classroom, and school noise (e.g., school bells, fire drills, hallway movement, cafeteria, and playground) may be difficult for new students to endure at first and impact their ability to learn.

Teachers should consider introducing elementary newcomers to classroom routines slowly with lots of repetition. Introduce vocabulary and new concepts both in print and visually through pictures, **realia**, and **TPR** (Total Physical Response). Pair the **newcomer** with another student ("classroom buddy"). Modify lessons to meet the student at his current learning level. Focus on key concepts for any new learning, and introduce new information by building a base of background knowledge that the newcomer has not experienced. When introducing sounds, letters, phonics, and word-building skills, remember that the newcomer has possibly not heard nor spoken English before entering the elementary classroom. In addition, even elementary teachers who have been trained to teach the basics of reading to a typical English learner may not think about the specific challenges of students with limited background knowledge due to interrupted schooling.

SPECIFIC CHALLENGES OF SECONDARY NEWCOMERS WITH LIMITED FORMAL SCHOOLING

While students of any age may enter U.S. schools with limited or even no previous education, the most critical challenges accompany students at the secondary level. By middle school, the type and amount of coursework carries with it the expectation that the student have a strong level of background knowledge of the subject (whether science, social studies, math, etc.) and a sufficient grasp of English to understand both the teacher and the text. Even in cases where there are courses available in the native language of the student, these courses will probably follow grade level expectations and are not designed to be remedial. And in many cases, bilingual classes are not an option, either because of funding, politics, or low numbers. Regardless of the cause of the problem, the result is the same. Interrupted education causes a serious disruption in the learning of the child. Students and teachers feel frustrated and overwhelmed, attempting to bridge what may at times seem like an unbridgeable gap.

In the final chapter of this book, we will offer some suggestions for programming and support for students with interrupted schooling, but first we look at why this is a particularly critical issue for adolescents.

A large-scale study published by Jorge Ruiz-de-Velasco and Michael Fix in 2000 studied the challenges faced by immigrant teens that arrive in the United States with significant gaps in their schooling. They looked at available research on this topic; then visited several schools where these students were enrolled. They found that

> many schools are admitting growing numbers of newcomer teen students who arrive in the United States with significant gaps in their formal schooling, having often been out of school for three or more years before entering this country. This trend is particularly evident in schools, like those we studied, that receive refugee students or proportionally large numbers of students from Mexico, Central America, and the Caribbean. Publicly supported schooling in many of those countries ends at the equivalent of 6th grade; in some countries adolescent students are only required to attend school part-time.

Schools rarely collect data on the immigrant student's prior school-ing, so it is not known how many underschooled newcomer teens there are in American schools. Nevertheless, data on **LEP** (limited English proficiency) students (which include first-generation new-comers as well as second-generation students) suggests that the number of underschooled LEP immigrants in secondary schools has grown significantly in the past two decades. One published estimate, for example, indicates that 20 percent of all LEP students at the high school level and 12 percent of LEP students at the middle school level have missed two or more years of schooling since age six. (Ruiz-de-Velasco & Fix, 2000, p. 46)

SPECIAL ACADEMIC PROGRAMMING MAY BE NEEDED FOR SIFE

Traditional programming for second language students, even specific courses for new arrivals, may not meet the unique needs of this popula-tion. Most bilingual and **ESL** (English as a Second Language) classes are meant to provide support and assist students to reach a level of language proficiency that they are able to be self-sufficient in academic classes. The focus is on developing the four domains of language: lis-tening, speaking, reading, and writing, while also filling in the gaps. For example, a ninth-grade ESL class might have students reading about events in American history to prepare them for their social stud-ies classes while at the same time building their reading skills. This would be adequate for students who need to further develop their reading skills, or for new arrivals who never took American history classes; but for students who have limited home language literacy or who have little or no English skills, this activity would be meaningless. They must first develop basic literacy, in their home language if possible, and definitely in English. For some students with no educational expe-rience, they may actually need to start with the basic concepts of print. Most ESL or bilingual heritage language classes are not prepared for students who are so far below grade level.

Other issues facing secondary newcomers with limited formal schooling involve the increasingly rigorous state standards that are in place across the country and the assessment-driven atmosphere of most school districts. Hopefully, with the newly authorized Elementary and Secondary Education Act of 2015 (known as Every Student Succeeds Act or ESSA) there will be some relief for SIFE, but much of the pressure to make years of progress in months will remain. And even where the external pressure is minimal, the students feel the pressure internally to catch up to peers and experience academic success. Especially for high school students, the need to earn credits, pass required graduation tests in many states, and prepare for post-secondary options often seem like insurmountable barriers.

Even in schools with specialized programming for SIFE, finding and training teachers to work with these students may pose a challenge. Secondary teachers are seldom trained to teach primary reading and math skills, while elementary level–trained teachers are not prepared to assist secondary students make the transition from basic skills to courses like algebra, physical science, or even high school language arts classes. Moving a student from learning the alphabet to reading an adapted version of Romeo and Juliet in one year takes a unique set of skills.

DeCapua, Smathers, and Tang talk about these issues in their book, *Meeting the Needs of Students with Limited or Interrupted Schooling* (2009). They state that

> [t]eachers—even ESL teachers—frequently lack adequate training because this population has specific literacy development and content-area knowledge needs that are markedly different from other **ELL**s [English language learners]. There is also a lack of textbooks and materials specifically designed for these students at the secondary level. Furthermore, most schools do not offer a clear support structure with teachers, guidance counselors, parent coordinators, social workers, and the families all involved. Finally, there is a lack of in-depth proven research on what works with **SLIFE** [students with limited or interrupted formal education]. (p. 4)

Even with all the barriers and challenges listed above, it is critical that teachers, schools, and school districts realize that with the proper support these students can succeed. As we will see in Chapter 4, students are resilient. Many of these students have overcome obstacles we cannot even imagine. They have faced challenges and moved on. They have a dream and will not give up, despite the difficulties. In a study on students with limited educational backgrounds, a team of researchers looked at what schools can do to help students with significant educational gaps, and they found strong, determined people with a drive to succeed. And they also saw that "even though most immigrant students with limited schooling have a lot of catching up to do, they can achieve at break-neck speed if the work begins at a level they can understand." (Mace-Matluck et al., 1998, p. 24) We, as educators, just need to provide the vehicle to put them on the track to success.

Another issue for older adolescents is the fact that they may literally run out of time to complete the requirements for high school graduation before the state-determined time to attend public school. This is especially true for students who come at age 16 or older without a transcript showing some completed high school courses. For most of these students, especially those with limited formal schooling, they not only have to learn English as quickly as possible, but they also do not have the content knowledge to move directly into rigorous academic courses like algebra or advanced science. Some schools offer remedial math or science class, and basic English proficiency courses, but the time they spend in these classes that may not count for high school graduation eats up valuable months or years. The students may "age out" of high school attendance and be forced into adult programs that also were not designed for their unique needs. All of these challenges contribute to the staggeringly high dropout rate mentioned earlier of up to 70% for recent immigrants with interrupted education (Fry, 2005).

In addition to the academic challenges faced by students with an interrupted education, many of these students are also dealing with emotional and social issues as well. Most refugee children and many Latinos, especially those who come as **unaccompanied minors**, have experienced serious traumatic events that are still having an impact on their ability to cope with the many changes in their lives. Many schools are not prepared to deal with these emotional and psychological needs even when the students share their situations; and many times, children are uncomfortable or even afraid to let others know about their personal lives. Chapter 4 will offer some suggestions for helping students build an inner **resilience** that can help them deal with and live through the upheaval in their lives; but some situations are so severe that counselors and other professionals may need to step in to provide additional support. In these cases, a support team can decide on the best type of assistance and where and how it can be provided.

CONCLUSION

As we have seen, the numbers of students entering our schools with limited or even no previous educational background is growing. In too many cases, the programming and services in place for English language learners is not adequate to meet their unique set of needs. The purpose of this book is to help raise the awareness of educators to the existence of this specific population, to explore the causes of interrupted education, to build empathy for their situation, and to offer practical support systems that can help these students not just survive, but succeed.

For Further Study

1. Does your school collect data on previous educational experiences for incoming students? If not, what could be added to the enrollment process to help identify students in need of additional services upon entrance?

2. Does your school or school district provide assistance to elementary students who have interrupted schooling? How is this program different for newly arrived elementary students from the traditional pull-out or push-in (co-teaching) or bilingual self-contained classes?

3. Does your school offer programming for newly arrived secondary students with interrupted education? How is this program different from the traditional ESL or bilingual courses?

4. Consider forming a study group in your school. Invite a representative sample of the members of your faculty, administration, child services team (school social worker, psychologist, etc.), paraprofessionals, and so on, to join the study group. Before beginning your work together as a study group, gather information/data about the English language population in your school, whether currently being served in an **English Language Development (ELD)** or bilingual program. As a study group,

   A. Set a regularly scheduled day and time to meet.

   B. Create a reading schedule calendar.

   C. Determine which "For Further Study" question(s) at the end of each chapter would be most beneficial for the teachers, administration, and paraprofessionals in your setting.

   D. Encourage study group members to work in partnerships to explore and report to the group. What will be the impact of this question on future programming, instruction, social, and interactional activities in our school?

2 LATINOS WITH INTERRUPTED EDUCATION

INTRODUCTION

Latinos are by far the largest linguistic minority in the United States, composing about 20% of the total population (Pew Research Center, 2013; U.S. Census, 2011). The term **Latinos** or **Hispanics** will be used somewhat interchangeably in this chapter, with Latinos being the larger population including anyone from Latin America, and with Hispanics referring only to the Spanish-speaking portion of the group. The phrase *Latin America* will encompass all the areas of North and South America in which Latin-based languages are spoken, predominately Spanish, but also French Creole and Portuguese.

Other than language heritage, the area represents extreme diversity in ethnicity, socio-economics, and educational opportunities. Some of the issues faced by new arrivals from this world area are common to several of the countries, while others are more particular to certain countries or areas. Attempts will be made to not overgeneralize, but to look at trends and concerns that some of the students from these countries bring with them as they enter U.S. schools. This chapter will focus on the issues that impact the education and social integration of new arrivals whose educational experiences in their home countries are affecting their academic success today.

The top Latin American countries represented in the continental United States, according to the Pew Research Center (2016), are listed in Table 2.1.

Table 2.1   Number of Latinos Living in the United States

Mexico	35,371,000
Puerto Rico (living in the U.S.)	5,319,000
El Salvador	2,100,000
Cuba	2,045,000
Dominican Republic	1,763,000
Guatemala	1,324,000
Colombia	1,046,000
Honduras	812,000
Haiti	616,000

Why Latinos Are Coming to the United States

As has been the case throughout history, people who are leaving their home country and culture are usually doing so for what is commonly termed either *push* or *pull* factors (Noguera, 2014, p. 295). Push factors are those that cause a person to leave because life has become difficult or even dangerous, such as war, natural disaster, or political upheaval. A pull factor is one that attracts **immigrants** such as economic or educational opportunity, religious or political freedom, or family ties. Immigrants from Latin America have chosen to come to the United States for a combination of both types of factors. Many of the countries listed above have experienced political or economic upheaval, and the resultant disarray has led many to flee to an area that offers physical or economic safety, often the United States. However, the political climate in the United States has not always been the most welcoming and peaceful for these new arrivals. Issues that can arise because of this dichotomy will be addressed later in the chapter.

These push and pull factors are especially strong for adolescent Latinos.

Many arrive without having experienced formal education in their countries of origin nor literacy in their native Spanish language. Consequently, there is growing evidence that immigrant youth are susceptible to a variety of hardships and pressures that many adults, including their parents, do not fully understand. These challenges and hardships encountered by Latino immigrant youth living in a society where hostility toward their presence is growing must be of concern to educators, service providers, and policymakers. . . . Many Latino immigrants leave to escape the ravages of political violence, to flee the suffering caused by unrelenting poverty, or in the wake of a natural disaster that has destroyed jobs, communities and possibilities for advancement. There are also those who come as political refugees to escape war, persecution, and torture. Even though they must overcome tremendous obstacles—barbed wire fences, coast guard vessels, or armed militias, they still come because for many, immigration offers the only possibility of hope. (Noguera, 2014, pp. 295–296)

Although most new arrivals face challenges, and must overcome social and well as physical barriers, it is the new arrivals from these countries with significant educational gaps that will be considered in this chapter. While it is possible to have students from Colombia and Cuba with interrupted educations, the percentages are so low (Lukes, 2015) that those countries will not be discussed in this chapter.

SITUATIONS AND CONDITIONS IN LATIN AMERICA THAT MAY CONTRIBUTE TO INTERRUPTED EDUCATIONS

Mexico

By far, the majority of Latinos in the United States have their roots in Mexico. Some are recent arrivals and others have a heritage in the United States that dates back to before the annexation of the Southwest by the growing nation more than 150 years ago. One reference to this heritage is the statement that for some Mexican-Americans, they crossed the border, but for others, the border crossed them.

It is impossible to look at the educational challenges of recent arrivals from Mexico without discussing the overwhelming impact of their immigration status. The percentage of Mexican-Americans immigrants who are undocumented is just over 50%. (It was 52% in 2012 and the percent has been declining for close to a decade, according to the Migration Policy Institute.) The implications of life in the shadows affect almost every aspect of life. In a recent study by Casteñada, Felt, Martinez-Taboada, Casteñada, and Ramirez (2013), it was found that more than half of young Mexican immigrants live in poverty or in near poverty. They also found that "[m]ore than any other group, Mexican immigrants have very little access to health insurance in the United States. In 2010, more than half (55%) of all Mexican immigrants living in the US did not have health insurance" (Casteñada et al., 2013, p. 70). And with adolescents, the percentage rises to 65%.

Another consequence of life "without papers" is the large number of students who are living with the uncertainly and fear this type of life generates. Young children, who often don't understand the concept of "authorized immigration status," will still be aware of the fear and anxiety that it causes. They may be afraid to leave home and go to school out of uncertainty of what may happen while they are gone, especially if they have witnessed the devastation of arrest and deportation of friends or family members. They may cling to the remaining family members, have nightmares, cry excessively, or have trouble eating and sleeping. Older youth may express their frustration and fear through depression, aggression, or rebellion at home or at school. And they may decide that rather than focus on the long-term, unsure benefits of an education, they will get a job and make as much money as possible while they can. When combined with the difficulties of being able to enter the post-secondary education world (which will be discussed later in the chapter), the allure of even a low-paying job is strong (Macias, 2015).

While not all undocumented immigrants are from Mexico, they definitely make up the largest percentage. In total, the

> Mexican unauthorized population stands at about 6.7 million, compared with about 500,000 for the next-largest source country (El Salvador), and as a group, unauthorized Mexicans have been in the country longer than others. Consequently, this group dominates the children of unauthorized immigrants. . . . The 450,000 U.S.-born children of unauthorized immigrants from Central and South America make up the next largest group. (Passel, 2011, p. 21)

While being undocumented does not equate to being categorized as students with interrupted formal education (SIFE), far too many Mexican-American students, especially adolescents, fit into both groups.

Educational System in Mexico

One of the major reasons children from Mexico make up a large percentage of students with interrupted schooling is the education system of Mexico. A recent book by Margarite Lukes (2015) titled *Latino Immigrant Youth and Interrupted Schooling: Dropouts, Dreamers, and Alternative Pathways to College* looks at the educational opportunities available in the home countries of many Latino students and discusses how those education systems contribute to the issues many of these children face. For example, she states that

> [c]ompulsory schooling in Mexico was limited to *primaria* or elementary school (six years) until 1993. In Mexico, nearly 17% of those between the ages of 12 and 15 have never attended school, while more than 25% do not finish the six compulsory years of school. Almost 50% of Mexicans leave school after elementary school and another 13% leave without finishing secondary education. Thus, nearly two thirds of the Mexican population do not complete nine years of education. (Lukes, 2015, p. 61)

This is especially true of students in rural or impoverished urban areas. The situation is compounded by the fact that

> students from Mexico may believe that they have completed their education upon finishing *la secundaria,* the equivalent of ninth grade in the U.S. because that is the end of compulsory education in Mexico. Upon immigrating to the U.S., these students may be unaware of the expectation to continue their education until the age of 18. (*Focus on SLIFE,* 2015, p. 1)

Since compulsory education ends with grade nine in Mexico, many students are confused and frustrated when they find out that U.S. laws and U.S. schools expect them to continue with their education until age 18. Additionally, many are expected to repeat grade nine because their transcripts may not indicate the completion of the typical grade nine courses for a U.S. high school. This is especially frustrating for the youth who choose to come to the United States to work, thinking they are ready for employment. One researcher stated that for many Mexican youth, this is *la edad para ir al norte*—"The age to go north" (Lopez Castro, 2005). These educational factors could contribute to the 60% dropout rate of Mexican immigrants (Cortina, 2009).

Many Mexican immigrants choose not to enroll in school when they arrive in the United States and enter directly into the workforce (Ruiz-de-Velasco & Fix, 2000). While they will obviously not be included in the dropout rate, they also will never obtain the all-important high school diploma and probably be relegated to low-wage jobs for life. In Lukes's study of Latinos in New York City, she found that Mexican immigrants have about a 40% nonenrollment rate, and it can be assumed that the percentage would be somewhat similar in other areas of the country. In a 2005 study by Fry for the Migration Policy Institute, the percentages are even more disturbing: Of recently arrived Mexican-born teens who did not keep up in school before coming to the United States, 83% were not enrolled in school. Hernandez, Denton, McCartney, & Blanchard (2012, p. 32) believe that "our education policy must address two very different populations, children for whom the education system has failed and adolescents and young adults who have never been touched by the US education system."

Work or School?

Recently, a door-to-door survey was conducted in an apartment complex in a Midwestern school district with a large Latino population. The desire was to identify school-age residents who would qualify for migrant assistance programs such as a summer tutoring and lunch program. The team conducting the survey returned to the school reporting that 12 teenagers, ranging in age from 13 to 18, had been discovered within just a few hours who had never enrolled in school since arriving in the United States. Ten were boys and two were girls, and all had chosen to obtain a job rather than enroll in school. Some stated that they didn't even realize that they were eligible for or permitted to attend school, or that it was required of teens in the United States. Some later enrolled, others simply disappeared.

How much of the high dropout rate of about 40%, as well as the non-enrollment rate, is caused by the pull to employment, how much is affected by the limited educational backgrounds and experiences before arrival, and how much is a result of the immigration status of these children is impossible to determine. Probably it is a combination of all of these factors and others as well. But schools need to be aware of these factors when dealing with Mexican immigrants and take these factors into consideration when planning curriculum and programming. Without immediate and drastic interventions, this new "underclass" of people in the United States will continue to grow—undereducated, living in poverty, and with limited or no access to health care.

Why is Mexican immigration declining?

While the number of immigrants from Mexico remain by far the largest nationality in the United States, the number and the percentage is actually on the decline. The number of recent immigrants from Mexico fell from 369,000 in 2005 to 125,000 in 2013, a 66% reduction in just eight years, according to the Census Bureau study. While legal immigration from Mexico declined slowly from 161,000 in FY 2005 to 135,000 in FY 2013, illegal migration fell much more rapidly. Southwest border appre-hensions of Mexican nationals, which indicate patterns of illegal entries, topped 1 million in FY 2005, falling to a historic low of 229,000 in FY 2014. Furthermore,

> [a] coincidental alignment of economic and demographic factors in both countries has spurred the decline in illegal immigration from Mexico. In the United States, the Great Recession significantly weakened the economy, and in particular depressed demand for low-wage workers, in construction and also in agriculture and other sectors that traditionally employ Mexican unauthorized workers. Equally important, the United States has significantly strengthened the immigration enforcement system in the past decade, making it more risky and costly to cross the border, and by deporting unauthorized immigrants quickly and in record numbers. (Chishti & Hipsman, 2015, p. 4)

While this pattern change will have an impact on schooling new arrivals in the United States, those who are already here and the significant numbers who are still arriving will continue to require specialized assistance. And while the number of recent immigrants from Mexico may be on the decline, the number of students from Central America is rising dramatically.

Central America (Guatemala, El Salvador, Honduras, Nicaragua)

Many people from Central America began arriving in the United States during and immediately after the civil wars that rocked Guatemala and El Salvador in the early 1980s. When it became evident that requesting **political asylum** from the bloody revolutions was not going to be granted, most chose instead to live undocumented (Zong & Batalova, 2015).

The economies of these two countries, and also that of neighboring Honduras and Nicaragua (after the fall of the Sandinistas), has led to unemployment rates of almost 50% and a precipitous rise of drug- and gang-related violence that has resulted in a mass exodus from these coun-tries. Some people are internally displaced, some have moved to more stable areas in Latin America, and thousands per year have trekked across Mexico to the Rio Grande border. Israel Medina (2014), a field psychologist who works with Doctors Without Borders, made this statement in an article found in *Forced Migration Review*:

> In some regions of these countries [El Salvador, Guatemala and Honduras], gang rule is absolute and young people are extremely vulnerable to forced recruitment into the gangs. Adolescents are continually intimidated and subjected to violence, pressurized into joining the gangs or working for them as drug pushers or in other roles. A recurrent theme in out-migration is the large number of children forced to leave their countries, exposing them to the dangerous conditions of the journey. Some families prefer to see their sons and daughters exiled rather than risk them being killed or forced into a life of crime. (p. 74)

An unprecedented number of emigrants from this violence-ridden area of the world are children. Those who make it to the southern border of the United States are overriding the ability of the legal and social services organizations to deal effectively with them. They have become known by their legal status as **unaccompanied minors** or unaccompanied alien children.

Who qualifies as an unaccompanied alien child?

An unaccompanied alien child is defined in the Homeland Security Act of 2002 as a child who (1) has no lawful immigration status in the United States; (2) has not yet attained 18 years of age, and (3) with respect to whom there is no parent or legal guardian in the United States available to provide care and physical custody. (Many educators prefer the term unaccompanied minors to the official term, UAC.)

Kids in Need of Defense, a non-profit organization that provides pro bono defense lawyers for these students, has recently published a document about the situation of these children. In a 2013 brief by KIND, they state that

> [t]he United States serves as a leading destination for thousands of children who migrate every year without a parent or legal guardian. They are escaping severe abuse and violence, persecution, extreme deprivation, and other human rights abuses such as female genital mutilation or forced marriage; others have been abandoned, or trafficked, and some are seeking work, hoping to go to school, or are trying to reunify with family members, many of whom had left the children behind years before. The children's

migration can also be, and very often is, the result of a combination of these factors. (*Understanding and addressing the protection of immigrant children who come alone to the United States*, 2013, p. 5)

While about 15% of the children that they serve are from other parts of the world, the vast majority are arriving from Central America.

A large percentage of this exodus are young people, some as young as 6 or 7. The number of unaccompanied children has increased dramatically in the last 10 years from less than 2,000 in 2004 to almost 60,000 in 2014. They travel singly or in groups, often traveling part of the way on the roof of the train known as the *La Beastia* (a cargo train that makes the journey from southern Mexico to near the northern border). Most of the children who are caught as they cross the border give violence in their home countries as their main reason they are seeking asylum in the United States. Others are coming to join family members who came before them or to find employment to be able to send money back to desperate family members.

> These children are given into the care of the Office of Refugee Resettlement, because they are asking for refugee asylum status. Most are united with family members or friends (90%), and some are kept in **ORR** [emphasis added] custody until some other placement is found (*Unaccompanied Alien Children U.S. Law and Policy Backgrounder*, 2014).

In a study prepared for Congress (Wasen & Morris, 2014) about the unaccompanied alien children arriving in FY2014, the following statistics were shared:

67% of the children were males and 33% females

25% were under the age of 12

38% were from Honduras

36% were from El Salvador

26% were from Guatemala

The recent wave of unaccompanied minors coming to the United States from Central America also generally fit into the SLIFE [students with limited or interrupted educational education] category. The violence and poverty that many of these young people experienced in their native countries have led to limited and interrupted educational opportunities. (*Focus on SLIFE*, 2015, p. 1)

In addition, the typical education provided for many of the students in Central America impacts their ability to adjust quickly to U.S. schools and be successful. As with Mexico, Honduras and El Salvador do not require attendance after Grade 9, while Guatemala has compulsory education until Grade 11. However, only about 60%–70% of the eligible students actually attend in each of these countries. And even when enrolled in school, attendance may be sporadic and the quality of the education varies depending on the length of the school day, the quality of the materials and the training of the teachers, and the facilities available for instruction (Lukes, 2015).

Some of these unaccompanied children have faced difficulty enrolling in school after arrival because they may not have an immediate family member with whom to be placed, being placed instead with a more distant relative or even into foster care. Guardianship issues have led to some schools refusing entry. A May 8, 2014, memo issued jointly from the U.S. Department of Justice and the U.S. Department of Education, in response to this situation, reminds school districts that no child may be denied admission to school based on immigration status, referring to the *Plyler v. Doe* Supreme Court decision of 1982. In the workshop mentioned above, the immigration lawyers giving the presentation stated that when contacted by families, they have directed school districts to enroll students as homeless as described in the **McKinney-Vento Act** if there is not yet legal guardianship established. This gives the families time to obtain the proper guardianship paperwork needed by the schools and allows the students to be enrolled immediately.

Teacher Resource Suggestions: Additional information for school district personnel is available on the internet in two documents: *Legal Issues for School Districts Related to the Education of Undocumented Children* (National Education Association and National School Boards Association, 2009) and *Unaccompanied Children in Schools: What You Need to Know* (2015).

Ricardo's Story

Ricardo is a 15-year-old boy from Honduras. He attended school for 4 years until he quit to help his mother work on the farm. His mother was killed when he was 12 and he moved in with an uncle. When he was 14, he was threatened by a local gang member and told that he would be shot if he did not join. Reluctantly, his uncle paid a **coyote** to help Ricardo escape and make the dangerous journey across Central America and Mexico to be reunited with a father he had never met. After 8 months, Ricardo crossed the border into Texas and was captured. He spent 2 months in a detention center until he was sent to Wisconsin to be with his father. Dad had since married and had other children, and the situation was uncomfortable and finally became untenable. He soon left dad and moved again to live with a cousin and uncle in a nearby state. Ricardo is now enrolled in a high school and struggling to fit in.

What types of academic and emotional supports will Ricardo need to be successful in his new setting?

Family Reunification Issues

Family reunification is extremely difficult when the family has been separated for so long. In a study conducted by the Harvard Immigration Project, 85% of immigrant children are separated from one or both parents sometime during the immigration process. For Central American children, the percentage rises to 96%, and the separation is of a much longer duration, and 80% of the time involved both parents (Suárez-Orozco, Suárez-Orozco, & Todorova, 2008).

These authors also are concerned at the

stunningly high proportion of newcomer students, both legal and illegal, who endure long separations from their parents is an issue of serious concern. Not only do the separations extract a high emotional cost for both parents and children, but they also often result in complicated and conflictual periods of adjustment when the family is finally reunited. (p. 375)

Furthermore, according to Rong and Priessle (2009), "Immigrant Central American children are more likely to have parents with fewer years of schooling and employment in menial jobs, to live in a linguistically isolated household, and to have English proficiency problems" (p. 245). They also have an extremely high dropout rate, almost twice the national average (p. 240).

While the number of minors who arrived in the United States during the fiscal year 2015 declined significantly to about half of the numbers in 2014, this still meant 30,000 new children entering U.S. schools with emotional issues to compound their academic challenges. And the numbers of unaccompanied alien children were back to the 2014 levels during the first half of fiscal year 2016.

Puerto Rico

The economy in Puerto Rico has been declining for almost two decades, and the impact of this is being felt in the education realm. One of the results of this economic decline has been the increase in people moving to the continental United States. The Pew Research Center says that this emigration is at its highest rate in 60 years, and it is affecting the number of students attending local Puerto Rican schools. The decline is so dramatic that there are about 40% fewer children in the schools than just 10 years ago (Krogstad, 2015). In fact, since the turn of the 21st century, there have been more Puerto Rican nationals living in the continental United States than on the island, and the trend continues.

As a result of this decline, educational funding from both Washington and San Juan has been cut. Schools that once had strong extracurricular activities and support services have been forced to cut back. Some of the incentives for secondary students to stay in school have disappeared at a time that the pressure to leave school and work to help support the family is growing. Some of these teens are choosing to move to the continental United States to look for work, but without first completing their high school diploma. And because they don't have the requirements to find a well-paying job in the United States, they either end up back in school with gaps in their education, are trapped in dead end jobs, or turn to drugs or crime for quick money.

Even students who have had consistent and uninterrupted education in Puerto Rico may have problems adjusting to the school system in the United States because their English is usually not at grade level. Many of the teachers in Puerto Rico teach reading and writing English as a subject, but instruction is in Spanish, and the students often have little opportunity to practice oral communication. (Personal interview with Sonia Colon, June 23, 2015, and Jose Luis Morales Crispin, July 21, 2015.)

Another consequence of the economic decline has been a shrinking of the salaries of teachers, which were already extremely low. Teachers are frustrated to see resources and student supports cut, leading to teacher strikes and work stoppages. All of these problems are leading to more students coming to U.S. schools on the mainland with interrupted educational experiences. (Personal conversation with Berena Cabarcas, principal of International Community High School in the Bronx.)

Implications for Teaching

In a study published in 2011 by Irizarry and Antrop-Gonzàlez, which focused on the factors leading to academic success for what they termed the "diasporicans," they found some exciting information. The researchers saw that teachers who respected the language and culture of the students, and who created a personal relationship with them, were able to encourage a positive attitude toward school, increasing attendance and academic engagement (pp. 249–254).

"Traditional notions of cultural capital also tend to define Puerto Rican students and others of diverse cultural backgrounds by who they are not and what they may lack, as opposed to who they are and what assets they bring to school" (p. 250). They quoted one teacher in their study as saying,

> Culture is a big thing that needs to be affirmed. My students feel very strong about being Puerto Rican. Kids need to keep who they are without being assimilated to American culture to be able to understand who they are as people. It is hard to define American culture, but basically, they shouldn't have to give up one culture for a new one. If you are going to work with people in any setting, you need to know their culture.

The teachers in this study saw their knowledge of and concern for the culture of their students as a "mutually enriching partnership," in which both the teachers and the students gained from the relationship.

Another factor in the perceived success of the students and teachers in this study was the willingness of the teacher to allow code-switching in the classroom [going back and forth between two languages], as well as the use of the home language and even "Spanglish" in the classroom to create an atmosphere of acceptance and empowerment. And finally, the students voiced their belief that their families and communities, including their religious institutions, gave them an inner strength to succeed (p. 250).

What teaching implications does this study have for working with other Latino students?

See Chapter 4, "Providing Social and Emotional Support: Developing Resilient Students" for additional suggestions for building resilience in SIFE.

Dominican Republic

The situation of students from the Dominican Republic is also strongly impacted by the educational system in their home country. Most immigrants come through the sponsorship of family members living legally in the United States. There are approximately 1.7 million Dominicans in the United States, with 1 out of 3 living in the New York metropolitan area (Nwosu & Batalova, 2014).

In this Caribbean nation of nearly 10 million people, the education system ranks among the worst in the world. . . . The Dominican Republic struggles with overcrowded classrooms in shoddy facilities. There's a high dropout rate, an outdated curriculum, overage students who fail classes and have to repeat grades, among other problems. But perhaps the most worrying issue is poorly trained teachers. . . . Across the country, about 40 percent of boys and girls leave school before eighth grade. Even those who get through high school and complete 12 years of school start college at a sixth-grade reading level, according to a Dominican university study. (Manning, 2014, p. 1)

Many students in the Dominican are not working at grade level and are required to repeat a grade because of excessive absences or broken enroll-ments. The issue of interrupted education is occurring even before the students leave and come to the United States. When these students arrive in the United States, their high rate of repeating grades due to excessive absence and poor attendance, often because of the economic demands that force children to work to support the family, impacts their academic suc-cess. "44% of Dominican elementary school students and 60% of second-ary students are older than average for their grade" (Lukes, 2015, p. 39). In addition to issues related specifically to education, many children have their education interrupted by the need to work.

This background of low expectations and interrupted schooling affects the children who arrive in the United States. Very few students are pre-pared for grade-level academic expectations even in their native Spanish, and when compounded with the necessity of learning English as quickly as possible to prepare for graduation, the barriers may seem insurmount-able. Lukes (2015), in her study of Latinos with interrupted schooling, calls for specialized programming for these students. With her focus on the education system in New York City, which is home to a substantial Dominican population, she saw the challenges that both the students and the schools face to meet the needs of students in the current political atmo-sphere with its inordinate focus on accountability. She states that

[t]he US has failed systemically and nearly without exception to cre-ate incentives for schools to serve students of high school age who have gaps in literacy, English proficiency and academic skills. The very system that was created to hold schools accountable for ensur-ing high achievement of all students has perpetuated a dogged deficit-oriented view of certain students. (Lukes, 2015, pp. 41–42)

Despite this negative climate, the education systems of both New York City and the state of New York are working on developing specific SIFE curriculum, material, and programming for these students, many of whom are from the Dominican Republic. Building literacy and content skills, while recognizing and acknowledging the culture and language capital of their students with limited schooling, are an attempt to not just keep students in school, but to allow them to reach their potential.

Haiti

Although Haiti shares the small island of Hispanola with its neighbor, the Dominican Republic, they have little else in common. The western third of Hispanola was given to the French in the 1600s, and rapidly became a wealthy colony with its economy based on the imported African slaves brought to work on the many plantations. In 1804, after a bloody struggle for independence, Haiti became the first black-led, post-colonial country in the world. The economy never fully recovered from the revolt, and today Haiti is the poorest country in the Western Hemisphere. Dictators and political disruptions were finally replaced by a democratically elected leader in 2004, only to be devastated by a powerful earthquake in 2010, reported to be the strongest in the region in the last 200 years. Because of the political and economic difficulties in the country, people have been emigrating to other Caribbean countries as well as attempting to come illegally to the southern coast of the United States for decades. Many have gone to their neighbor, the Dominican Republic, for work and safety. Recently, the government of the Dominican Republic has decided that any undocumented Haitians are going to be aggressively found and deported, leading to strikes and protests. At the time of the writing of this book, the situation remains strained and unresolved.

For those families who make it to the United States, their reception is slightly more welcoming. Following the earthquake of 2010, the government decided to allow Haitian immigrants to apply for Temporary Protective Status **(TPS)**, allowing them to remain until conditions improve in Haiti. According to the Migration Policy Institute, there are about 600,000 Haitians in the United States, with the overwhelming majority living in Miami, New York City, Boston, Orlando, and Atlanta.

> Surveys conducted by the UNDP [United Nations Development Program] indicate that Haitians who are 25 years and older received on average only 4.9 years of education and only 29 percent attended secondary school. These statistics show that a generation of Haitian youth is at risk for not having the necessary knowledge and basic skills to succeed in the labor force and contribute to the continued development of the country. Most schools in Haiti have minimal government support, lack qualified instructors, and are relatively expensive. More than 80 percent of primary schools are privately

managed by nongovernmental organizations, churches, communities, and for-profit operators, with minimal government oversight. School expenses are often a significant financial burden for low-income families. Half of public sector teachers in Haiti lack basic qualifications and almost 80 percent of teachers have not received any pre-service training. (USAID.gov website, 2014)

TYPICAL ISSUES OF LATINO SIFE AND RECOMMENDATIONS FOR EDUCATORS

While Latino students attending U.S. schools may have varied national backgrounds and may even speak different languages, there are some similarities in their experiences and their challenges. Listed below are some of the barriers that may contribute to the high dropout rate and lower academic achievement seen in many of these students. Recommendations will be provided, which may help ameliorate these barriers, providing support that will help students stay in school, graduate, and be prepared for life after high school.

Attendance

The poor attendance rate of some Latino students can be attributed to a number of key factors. Because many families are working in low-paying, minimum wage jobs, they may have to work more than one job to make enough money to support the family. Adolescents, especially girls, are often needed at home to care for young children so that parents are able to work. If a young child is sick, parents may not have the option of staying home. And when the children know more English that the parents, they may be needed as translators for appointments. Young men may be needed to help the older men at a construction or landscaping job, or they may be required to work day hours at their regular night job. Many teenagers work late hours and find the early hours of a typical high school impossible to maintain.

Another reason for disrupted attendance is the desire for families to maintain strong ties with relatives who remain in the home country. Often this results in the entire family returning for an extended Christmas vacation, or to sending children back home to care for aging relatives or to maintain the home language and culture. Pedro Noguera, in his study, states, "Finding ways to help reduce the strains caused by separation, while minimizing the losses in learning associated with the extended absences, is an important pedagogical consideration for schools that serve large populations of Latino immigrant youth" (Noguera, 2014, p. 296).

Limited Postsecondary Options

The ability to attend college is a huge issue for undocumented students. As of 2009, only nine states permitted undocumented students to receive in-state tuition rates according to the National Immigration Law Center. In 2012, President Obama issued an executive order now known as **DACA** (Deferred Action for Childhood Arrivals) that temporarily allowed undocumented students to attend college and get jobs. Since the implementation of DACA, the number of states who allow in-state tuition for undocumented students has risen from 9 to 24 (*Deferred Action for Childhood Arrivals*, 2014). At the time of the writing of this book, there continues to be controversy and uncertainty over the future of this program. Repeated attempts to declare this executive action illegal have been unsuccessful, leaving these students in limbo yet again.

DACA was a reaction to the frustration over the inability of Congress to pass a version of the DREAM Act, which has been discussed and debated for several years. The DREAM Act (Development, Relief, and Education of Alien Minors Act) would have allowed undocumented children to attend college, join the military, and gain legal employment. Despite numerous attempts to draft and pass this legislation, it has not gotten the majority of legislators behind it that would be required for passage.

DACA is an acronym for an executive order given by President Barack Obama in June 2012 to assist young people who arrived in the United States before 2007 and who were currently attending school or who had previously graduated. It allowed these students to be free from deportation, obtain a work permit, and in half of the states attend college at in-state tuition rates. It also allowed them to join the armed forces (see box below) and in most states, obtain a driver's license. It is not a path to citizenship, but it does provide a future for these students, even if only in the short term. (For more information on DACA and the DREAM Act, visit the National Immigration Law Center at nilc.org.)

Suggestions for Supporting DACA Students

School employees, and especially high school counselors, need to familiarize themselves with the impact of DACA in their own state. Some school districts are not allowing students who had previously left school to return and complete high school, in violation of their rights to an education. More states are allowing in-state tuition each year, and some are even permitting state financial aid to be

(Continued)

(Continued)

available to undocumented students. Legal action to allow "DACAmented" students to join the military is hoping to open those doors soon as well. With driver's licenses available in most states and many colleges open to undocumented students, DACA is providing students with more reason than ever to stay in school and graduate.

Impact of Immigration Status

As mentioned earlier in this chapter, the impact of immigration status for many Latinos cannot be overemphasized. Aside from students from Puerto Rico, who are U.S. citizens, a significant number of students from many of the other Latin American countries are not in the U.S. legally. For many of the other students, the possibility of coming through legal channels is remote if not virtually impossible. In addition to the stress of uncertainly about limited opportunities to life after high school, living with the constant threat of discovery and deportation affects almost every aspect of life while still in school.

When thinking about the impact on children of their or their parents' immigration status, the authors of *Learning a New Land* ask this question: "Are we willing to pay the price of having nearly two million children and youth living in the shadows, sentenced to managing life as undocumented immigrants? . . . Our challenge is to make sure that they will one day be able to better themselves and contribute to their new society" (Suárez-Orozco, Suárez-Orozco, & Todorova, 2008, p. 375). This belief mirrors the landmark Supreme Court decision that opened the doors to elementary and secondary education to anyone living in the United States.

Plyler v. Doe–1982
Supreme Court Decision

In 1982, the Supreme Court announced its decision on a case overturning a Texas law in which school districts would receive funds only for the education of children legally in the country. This decision, known as *Plyler v. Doe,* found that school districts must not consider a child's immigration status a factor for enrollment. In the majority opinion, written by Justice Douglas, the court stated that because "the illegal alien of today may well be the legal alien of tomorrow," and that without an education, these undocumented children, who are already at a disadvantage as a result of poverty, lack of English-speaking ability, and undeniable racial prejudices "will become permanently locked into the lowest socioeconomic class." He continued by writing,

> By denying these children a basic education, we deny them the ability to live within the structure of our civic institutions, and foreclose any realistic possibility that they will contribute in even the smallest way to the progress of our Nation.

Poor Educational Opportunities in the Home Countries

An extensive study of the educational experiences of Latino immigrants was conducted by Marguerite Lukes and published in 2015. One of the most compelling components of her study was a chart listing how many years of compulsory education is required in many Latin American countries and what percentage of the eligible population actually attends. This information helps educators in the United States to understand why so many of our Latino students are ill-prepared for the academic challenges of secondary school.

The total educational picture of students from Latin America must also include the type of education being received in the school when attending. "Quality of schooling is a moving target and includes factors such as time spent in the classroom, quality of materials, instructional design, teacher quality and academic achievement and literacy levels" (Lukes, 2015, p. 59).

Table 2.2 Years of Compulsory Education in Latin America

Country	Years Required	Percentage Actually Attending Final Grade
U.S.	12	96
Colombia	9	43
Ecuador	9	40
El Salvador	9	23
Dominican Republic	9	60
Mexico	9	28
Honduras	9	21
Guatemala	11	no data

Source: Lukes (2015)

Dr. Lukes (2015) continues her comments on the role of prior education for new arrivals with her statement:

> Key to understanding the academic progress of immigrant students—the challenges they face and their success—is the research-based finding that among students learning English as a second (or third or fourth) language, those with a more solid academic grounding in their home language have a much easier time both learning English and learning new academic context and skills. (Burt and Peyton, 2003). . . . As a result, students with gaps in their education in the home language tend to struggle and make limited progress in learning English. (p. 64)

The importance of first language literacy is documented through numerous studies, and most well known are the decades of records reviewed by the husband and wife team of Wayne Thomas and Virginia Collier. Thomas stated in a Columbus, Ohio presentation in 2014 that together they had looked at close to a million school records over a period of 25 years since their initial 1989 study, and the evidence was overwhelming that students with first language literacy surpassed their peers in academic proficiency. Their research was affirmed by the meta-study, conducted by August and Shanahan in 2006, which showed that when students are literate in their native language and have developed sufficient reading and writing skills in that language, they can more easily apply that knowledge to the new language. Conversely, "school leaders should anticipate that students from non-literacy-oriented homes, with interrupted prior school experiences, and/or who are living in poverty will likely take much longer than high-achieving, literacy-oriented, socioeconomically advantaged students" (Zacarian, 2011, p. 25). The difficulty of building and/or maintaining first-language literacy is compounded by the fact that for some students from rural Mexico or Guatemala, Spanish is not their first language. They speak an indigenous language, and sometimes the students may know little or even no Spanish.

Implications of Limited Educational Opportunities Before Arrival

While educators in the United States cannot control the education received by students before they enter our doors, we must find ways to build on the educations already received. Some students will need less support to make the transition, but many have significant gaps that can only be overcome with specialized curriculum and programming. Bilingual courses can help students understand complex material while their English skills develop, and ESL classes are necessary to build that critical English proficiency. Sheltered courses are needed for students with some content background who need additional support while transitioning to English instruction. And for the students with the least educational backgrounds, newcomer programs and special SIFE classes are crucial. With time and the proper support, these students can reach their potential and become contributing members of their society.

See Chapter 5, "Providing School-Based Supports for SIFE," for expanded descriptions of recommended support systems.

Higher Dropout Rates

National statistics show a 33% dropout rate for Latinos born outside the United States, with a dropout rate 6 times that of white students and 3 times that of blacks, and also 3 times the rate of their U.S.-born Latino peers (Lukes, 2015).

Statistics also show a staggeringly low college attendance and completion rate. This low number can partly be explained by the high Latino dropout rate. Students who don't complete high school will not be eligible to attend postsecondary programs. Another factor in this low college attendance rate, and probably also in the high school dropout rate, was that before DACA, students without legal status often could not attend college in their home state without paying exorbitant international rates. According to Abrego (2014), these rates are often 3 to 7 times the in-state rate. With little incentive to stay in school and graduate, some students chose to leave school and begin working as soon as they felt they were old enough. In a report published by the Education Trust in 2003, it was stated that both college enrollment and completion rates had not increased in the previous 20 years, and "out of every 100 Latino kindergarteners, only 11 will obtain at least a bachelor's degree." However, by 2014 the same organization was able to report that the college graduation rate had increased to 16%; still too low but moving in the right direction.

This high dropout rate can be attributed to several causes: immigration status and its myriad implications, the pull to choose work over education, frustration over falling behind academically, inability to pass state-mandated graduation tests, and for some girls, pregnancy and motherhood. Two researchers, Noguera and Lukes, have focused their studies on the education of Latino adolescents. Pedro Noguera looked at the data surrounding the dropout rates of Latinos and found that they are the ethnic group most likely to dropout, the most likely to have children as teenagers, and the least likely to attend college.

And the dropout rates are not limited to undocumented teens from Mexico and Central America. The number of Puerto Rican students who do not complete high school is over 50%, and the number of Dominicans is just over 40% (Lukes, 2015, p. 7). Furthermore, all Puerto Rican and most Dominicans are in the United States legally, so their immigration status is not usually the issue.

Employment Issues

Many Latinos from each of the countries listed above come to the United States primarily for employment. Some come to make money to help support family members back home through remittances, some come to support the families that accompany them on the journey, and others felt that their opportunities for advancement or even making a decent living wage were limited in their native environment. Whatever the reason, employment can interfere in the education process in many ways. As mentioned earlier, many youth choose to get a job and never enroll in school upon arrival. Others try to work and go to school at the same time, often working late at night and then coming to school with not enough sleep and no time to have completed homework or studied for tests. Whatever the particular situation, employment cannot be ignored as a factor in educating Latino youth dropping out to work. (Fry, 2005, p. 1).

Especially vulnerable are the teens that come without a strong educational background. Fry found that 40% of the students who came with prior educational difficulties, including being overage for their grade level or having dropped out before emigrating, were most likely to be working in agriculture or construction.

Trauma

Another challenge that faces many adolescent immigrants, not just those with interrupted schooling, is the emotional strain of leaving one's home country behind. This is difficult for all immigrants; but for many of Latino students, it involves a dangerous and potentially deadly journey, often undertaken alone or with other minors.

> Undocumented immigrants can encounter a variety of dangers at the border including heat exhaustion, drowning, rape, and other forms of violence. These experiences can lead to severe posttraumatic symptoms as well as feeling that range from mild sadness to depression. Boys who have experienced trauma tend to exhibit greater levels of anger and depression than girls, but these symptoms usually decline over time. Girls who have had

traumatic experiences associated with immigration, while they do better academically than boys on average, report more psychosomatic complaints the longer they are in the new homeland. . . .

Undocumented students are particularly at risk as a result of their unstable legal status. Once settled, they may continue to experience fear and anxiety about being apprehended, being again separated from their parents, and being deported. Such psychological duress can take its toll on their academic performance and engagement in school. In addition, undocumented students with dreams of graduation from high school and going on to college may find that their legal status stands in the way of their access to post-secondary education. When immigrant adolescents know this reality while still in high school, it can affect their engagement with learning. (Suarez-Orozco, Qin, & Anthor, 2008, pp. 55–56)

Voices from the Field

An administrator in a high school reported frequent symptoms of self-mutilation or cutting and eating disorders by Latino girls and high rates of depression by both sexes. The majority of potential suicides by the students at the school overwhelmingly involved Latino girls. Although the root causes of these dramatic reactions to trauma was not clear, the problem was compounded by the fact that most had no health insurance. Finding professional long-term counseling for these adolescents was very difficult. Some clinics would work with the students for immediate, emergency situations; but finding organizations and health care professionals who could provide assistance to the teen and their family over a period of time was almost impossible.

Limited Academic Home Support

For a number of reasons already listed above, many Latino parents are able to provide only limited support for homework. They may have limited educational backgrounds themselves, think that their English skills are insufficient to provide the necessary assistance, or may be working in the evening and weekends. They may be embarrassed to approach the teacher or they may believe that the language and cultural barriers are too great. And because high school in the United States is so very different from secondary school in many Latino countries, students and their parents often do not know what is necessary to prepare for post-secondary options. For all of these reasons, parents often feel unequal to the task.

"Immigrant Latino youth often find themselves caught between two worlds, neither fully American, nor fully part of their parent's country" (Noguera, 2014, p. 295). This can cause tension and conflict between the adolescent and their parents, not unlike that of any teenager, but with the additional layer of language and culture loss. With the added challenges of patchy previous schooling, the pressure to work and earn money for the family, and limited legal options after graduation for the undocumented, it is understandable why so many Latinos dropout of school in frustration.

CONCLUSION

As educators, we must stay knowledgeable of state and national policies that are impacting our students. This knowledge will assist us as we open the doors to the future. We want to ensure that all students are prepared to walk through those doors with the skills and knowledge that will enable them to contribute to our society and fulfill that dream that brought them to the United States.

For Further Study

Form a study group in your school or school district to discuss the implications of interrupted education on the students in your area. Use the questions below to guide your discussions.

1. What themes were prevalent in this chapter on the causes and implications of limited previous schooling for Latino students? Are these themes present in your school's newcomer population? What action plan can be developed to address these issues?

2. Whose responsibility is it in your school district to identify, and if possible, enroll students who are not attending school? Has a concerted effort been made to find and enroll missing Latino students?

3. What programming options could be implemented to increase the attendance rate of Latinos and to ameliorate issues such as those listed above?

4. What is the impact of living undocumented, limited legal postsecondary options, and limited access to health care (including dental, vision, and mental health support) on Latino students in your school or school district? What programs does your district currently have to support these students? What could your school do better to assist undocumented students?

5. What are the potential implications for students who are not living with parents or guardians? Form a study group of key school personnel (teachers, counselors, administrators, etc.) to read and discuss *Enrique's Journey* by Sonia Nazario, a true account of an unaccompanied minor. After reading, discuss the following questions: Do you know whose responsibility is it at your school to find out which students need extra support because of these types of situations? How can a school find out about home issues without invading a student's privacy?

6. What is the impact of school accountability and standards-based education on Latino SIFE in your school setting?

7. What effect does the economic and political chaos of a student's home country (such as Haiti or Honduras) have on school-age immigrants?

8. What is your state or school district doing to cut the dropout rate for Latinos and to encourage them to stay in school?

9. What can schools do to aid Latino parents in their efforts to provide academic home support?

10. We do not control the situations our students have experienced before coming to our schools, or the political and legislative world in which we and our students now live; but as educators, it is our responsibility to see that each student reaches their fullest potential. With the information you received in this chapter, how can you now better serve the students in your classroom?

Vignettes

Review the following vignettes of the types of issues you may experience when serving Latino children with an interrupted education. Think about the background of each child, what he or she may have experienced that could have contributed to their current situation, and what academic programming and social services may be needed to help this child thrive.

Luis is a 15-year-old boy who recently arrived from El Salvador. He completed the compulsory 9 years of schooling in San Salvador with average grades. He came to the United States to live with his father who came to California almost 10 years ago. During that time, the father has remarried and has two more children. Luis is having a difficult time adjusting to his new home life and his new school.

Marie is an 8-year-old from Haiti. She is very small for her age, possibly due to malnutrition. She attended school sporadically for 1 year in Haiti before her family came to Boston where they are pursuing asylum. Marie is quiet and speaks only when spoken to, even in her native Creole. Her academic skills in both reading and math are mid-kindergarten level.

Beatriz is a 12-year-old girl from Honduras who came to the United States with her 14-year-old brother. They were detained at the border and spent about 2 months in a shelter in southern Texas before being united with an aunt in Chicago. Both children have mid-elementary level academic skills and attendance issues. Social workers at the school have experienced difficulties connecting with the aunt to discuss the school situation of both students.

Lidia is the 12-year-old daughter of a Mexican migrant family who moved to Virginia from the Carolinas. The family has settled in northern Virginia, but years of moving has impacted her ability to feel comfortable and make friends. Her spoken English is almost native-like, but she reads at a second-grade level. Her teachers have recommended her for intervention in the RTI process.

Juan is a 10-year-old recent arrival from Cuba where his family is uniting with grandparents who live in the Miami area. He completed 3 years of school in Cuba, but was pulled from school when the parents received word that they were coming to the United States. He has no English proficiency, but basic skills in Spanish and math.

3 UNIQUE ISSUES OF REFUGEE CHILDREN

INTRODUCTION

The second largest group of students who enter U.S. schools with interrupted educations are refugee children. Often these students have the greatest gaps in their education, and they sometimes arrive with no previous educational experience. In this chapter, we will look at how refugee status is determined, who protects refugees, and how they are selected for resettlement. We will also look at how life in a refugee camp can lead to interrupted education, and provide some information on the major cultural groups who have been resettled in the past few years.

REFUGEES AND RESETTLEMENT

A **refugee** is someone who "owing to a well-founded fear of being persecuted for reasons of race, religion, nationality, membership in a particular social group, or a political opinion' is outside the country of their nationality and cannot return" (Convention Relating to the Status of Refugees, 1951). The United Nations, through their division known as the High Commission on Refugees **(UNHCR)**, is the organization that has been tasked with the responsibility to protect and assist refugees. They interview potential individuals who claim to be refugees, create and support refugee camps in areas of flight, and oversee refugee **repatriation** or resettlement.

There are three possible futures for refugees, also known as **"durable solutions"**: voluntary repatriation back to the home country, local integration into the country of flight, and resettlement into a third country.

Only about 1% of all refugees a year are resettled into a third country. Typically, about 100,000 refugees worldwide are resettled each year through normal channels. No one knows how the unprecedented migration and resettlement of Syrian refugees will ultimately affect the resettlement process, with nearly a million asylees entering Europe in 2015.

After a period of years in a camp, refugees may become eligible for resettlement. There is no definite timeline, since the resettlement is a negotiated process with the receiving countries. Most refugees wait at least 5 years before they are considered for resettlement. Resettlement involves the selection and transfer of refugees from the country where they have sought refuge to a new country that has agreed to admit them—as refugees—with permanent residence status. This status

> ensures protection against **refoulement** [emphasis added; being forced to return to the home country] and provides a resettled refugee and his/her family or dependents with access to rights similar to those enjoyed by nationals. Resettlement also carries with it the opportunity to eventually become a naturalized citizen of the resettlement country. (Refugee Resettlement Trends, 2015, p. 5)

Numbers vary on the total number of refugees worldwide, but according to the official UNHCR figures, there were 14.5 million refugees at the end of 2014. They report that the global refugee population has doubled since 2010 and grew another 25% in 2014 (UNHCR, 2014, p. 2). Due to the

Table 3.1 Top 10 Home Countries of Refugees in 2013

1. Afghanistan	2,500,000
2. Syria	2,400,000
3. Somalia	1,100,000
4. Sudan and South Sudan	600,000
5. DR Congo	500,000
6. Myanmar	479,000
7. Iraq	400,000
8. Colombia	397,000
9. Vietnam	300,000
10. Eritrea	308,000

Source: UNHCR Statistical Online Population Database, 2014.

Syrian crisis, that number may be as large as 18 million by the end of 2015. Listed below (Tables 3.2–3.4) are statistics about where these refugees are coming from, where they are being resettled, and what languages they speak. Statistics are often up to 2 years behind due to a number of reasons.

Table 3.2 Top 10 Home Countries by Percentage Being Resettled in 2015

Myanmar	27%
Iraq	19%
Bhutan	12%
Somalia	12%
DR Congo	7%
Afghanistan	4%
Eritrea	3%
Syria	3%
Iran	3%
Sudan	2%

Source: Refugee Resettlement Trends, 2015, p.2.

Table 3.3 Top 10 Countries of Resettlement and the Number of Refugees Accepted

United States	59,548
Australia	10,691
Canada	9,160
Germany	4,775
Sweden	2,456
Norway	1,202
Netherlands	1,029
Finland	929
New Zealand	894
United Kingdom	710

Source: UNHCR Global Resettlement Statistical Report for 2013, 2014.

Table 3.4 Top Five Languages of Refugees Resettled in the United States Between 2008 and 2014
• Arabic
• Nepali
• Somali
• Karen (from Burma)
• Spanish

Source: Served Populations by State and Country of Origin, 2016.

Refugee Resettlement Process in the United States

Each year, the UNHCR provides the total number of refugees that will be accepted by each receiving country. The number to be resettled in the United States is determined by the Department of State before the beginning of the new federal fiscal year, which is October 1. That number for the past 10 years has been around 60,000 a year. However, the current Syrian crisis has resulted in temporarily increased numbers. The number of refugees accepted in the US rose to 110,000 in fiscal year 2016. Refugees are interviewed in the camps to determine their eligibility based on need, clearance by Homeland Security, and health status.

Refugee resettlement is run through the Office of Refugee Resettlement, which is a division of the U.S. Department of Health and Human Services. There are nine national resettlement agencies (with 315 local affiliates in 180 communities) that are authorized to resettle refugees across the country. Local arms of these agencies (see below) actually do the work of resettlement in whatever city they are located.

Hebrew Immigrant Aid Society

International Rescue Commission

World Relief

United States Conference of Catholic Bishops

Ethiopian Community Development Council

Lutheran Immigration and Refugee Services

Episcopal Migration Ministries

U.S. Committee for Refugees and Immigrants

Church World Service (an umbrella organization of several Protestant denominations)

These local agencies, which are commonly lumped together under the acronym of **VOLAG (voluntary local agencies)** do the onsite resettlement. They are responsible for the following:

- Meet refugees at the airport
- Find them housing, clothing, and household goods
- Help them apply for cash, medical, and food stamp assistance from local state agencies
- Arrange for their comprehensive health screening
- Enroll them in classes to learn English, American culture, work skills, and eventually the skills and information needed to pass the citizenship test
- Help them overcome problems and barriers to successful employment and integration into American life

Refugees get direct support from the Department of State through the individual states to the VOLAGs for the first 90 days and then possibly additional time, which varies by state. Typically, financial and other types of support (English and employment classes, health care) may last up to 8 months, depending on need and state assistance. Most refugees qualify for government support based on the same criteria as native-born citizens, unlike immigrants who are barred from receiving any type of financial assistance. After 5 years, refugees are eligible to apply for citizenship. One stipulation of their resettlement is that refugees must repay the cost of their flight back to the U.S. government.

It is usually personnel from these agencies, often the family's case-worker, who are responsible for helping children in the family get registered for school. Many refugee children will only have an **I-94** instead of the typical birth certificate. An I-94 is the document all refugees receive that shows they have authorization to enter the United States. As refugees, they have all the rights of citizens except voting, and they may petition to become citizens within a few years. Some I-94s are just pieces of paper like white cardstock; others are more durable and have a photo. They have a number, a birthdate, the individual's name, and the country of origin. Usually this document is replaced with a **"green card"** within about a year, which serves as identification until a person becomes a citizen. Most children, even if they attended school in the camp, will not have school paperwork or transcripts.

Cultural Orientation

Cultural Orientation (CO) is the training that refugees receive just before they move on to whatever third country is accepting them for resettlement. Each country has its own cultural orientation because it is an opportunity for the families to find out about life and services in their new home. In the 1980s, when refugees were predominately people from Southeast Asia and Eastern Europe, the typical CO period was between 6 and 18 months; now the pre-arrival training ranges from 1 to 5 days. Today's CO covers 11 major areas: predeparture processing (including how to ride on an airplane), role of the resettlement agency, housing, employment, community services, education, health, transportation, money management, the rights and responsibilities of refugees, and cultural adjustment (Costello & Bebic, 2006). This training can vary from between 2 to 30 hours. With this amount of time available, obviously the majority of CO must now occur after the individuals arrive in the United States, at the same time they are learning English and preparing for employment. While adults receive their cultural orientation as part of the resettlement process, children are left to receive whatever training a school system is prepared to provide.

EDUCATIONAL CHALLENGES FOR REFUGEE CHILDREN

Education is a basic human right for all children, and it is especially important that refugee children receive schooling because it creates a sense of security and hope, which is often lacking in refugee settings. . . . Education teaches self-reliance, helps create the human social capital needed for development, and plays a fundamental role in providing both physical and psychosocial protection for the child. Education is also critical for refugee children, so that they can be informed about health and hygiene. . . .

While overall refugees value education and realize it is important for their children, basic survival in the camps often takes precedence. Girls may be needed for gathering firewood, fixing food, or childcare. Without strict regulations on who must attend, children may choose to find other activities to fill their day. And those who attend school often face upheaval as children and teachers alike join and leave the school due to repatriation or new influxes of refugees, making an educational experience unstable and constantly changing. (Unite for Sight website, n.d.)

Typical Education in a Refugee Camp

Education in refugee camps is provided through a joint effort between UNHCR and whatever governmental agencies have a presence in each camp. In a report on schooling in refugee camps (*Refugee Education in*

2002/2003, 2003), there were 250 refugee camps worldwide in 22 countries. UNHCR funded about two-thirds of the schools and teachers in the camps, and local governments and other organizations provided the remaining one third. About 33% of the camp schools had only open-air classrooms, with no permanent buildings; but in some countries, the percentages were much higher. In Nepal, the percentage rose to 88%, while in Thailand, all classes were held outdoors.

The recommended teacher load is 40 students per teacher, but less than half the schools have been able to meet this goal. The camps with the largest average class sizes are mainly in Africa: Dadaab (70:1) and Kakuma (80:1) in Kenya, Tanzania (100:1), Guinea (75:1), and Uganda (68:1).

This report also looked at the enrollment statistics by gender and found that the percentage of girls enrolled in school in all camps is about 45% at primary level, but drops to 25% after Grade 6. And this includes only the girls who actually enroll. No one knows how many never enrolled. A more recent study of a camp in Jordan (Za'atari) that serves almost 800,000 Syrian refugees found that 76% of the girls and 80% of the boys between 6 and 18 years old do not attend school. Rates of school attendance are at the same low level for girls and boys in primary school, but drop even lower for boys at the secondary school level (*Shattered Lives,* 2013).

According to parents, the main reason why children do not attend school is lack of interest. They also cite family expectations of returning soon to Syria and violence against children en route to and from school. However, the majority of primary and secondary school-aged children themselves report that they would like to go to school. They say their key reasons for nonattendance (or dropping out) are violence and harassment en route to and from school and between students at school, corporal punishment, insecurity about leaving their family even for a few hours, having to help at home or work to earn money, the distance to school, and the lack of appropriate toilets (*Shattered Lives,* 2013, p. 18).

The situation is similar in other camps. In Dadaab, another mega-camp with nearly one-third million individuals, about 42% of the primary age children were attending school, and less than 5% of the secondary age students were enrolled (*Health Concerns in Ethiopia Camps,* 2011). In addition to the poor attendance rate of the children, another factor that causes limited educational skills of refugee children is the poor quality of many of the teachers. For example, in the Dadaab study, in the years between 2006 and 2010, there were 1,933 active teachers, but only 142 were trained. To meet the needs of the number of children in the camps, another 5,500 teachers would need to be hired and trained (p. 7).

The educational situation in refugee camps is obviously one of the major causes of students coming to their resettled countries with little or no formal education. While no formal study has been done of the total percentage of school-age students who fit into the SIFE category upon arrival, the Migration Policy Institute in Washington, DC, based on data from the American Community Survey (a periodic survey conducted by the U.S. Census Bureau in 2014), found that adult refugees coming to the United States had the following levels of education:

Percent of adults who are literate in their home language upon arrival:

Hmong	18%
Somalis	25%
Liberians	33%
Bhutanese	38%

It would be logical to assume that percentages of literacy for school-age children would be similar, if not lower.

Challenges Facing Refugee Students in Primary and Secondary Education

> Admittedly, teaching students who are refugees is challenging, particularly at the secondary level in light of high-stakes testing, curricular standardization, and the many diverse students for whom teachers are accountable. This is further exacerbated considering refugee students might lack formal education or second-language skills to effectively communicate when translators are not available. Refugee students often come from backgrounds and worldviews that are vastly different from their teachers', making it difficult, if not nearly impossible, for secondary teachers to single-handedly learn about all of their students' past and present experiences, cultures, and languages or how to best nurture their learning. (Stewart, 2015, p. 150)

Refugee students with interrupted or limited formal education face particular difficulties in adjusting to U.S. schools. Many refugee children arrive in the United States after prolonged stays in refugee camps where opportunities for schooling were limited or unavailable as was discussed earlier. In addition to the typical **culture shock** experienced by new arrivals, adjusting to the rigors of secondary school adds another layer of frustration. Students are usually placed by age, not academic skills (a practice we definitely encourage), but this also increases the gap between what students are capable of doing and what they are expected to do.

SUPPORT FOR REFUGEE CHILDREN

What types of services do refugee children require upon arrival?

Most refugee children come with typical issues that fall into four main categories: School Socialization, Academic, Social Needs, and Physical/Emotional Health. Following is a list of the types of challenges that refugee children face.

School Socialization Issues

- Lack of knowledge of school culture and accepted norms
- Inability to concentrate for extended periods of time
- Inability to work in groups successfully
- Unaware of necessity for consistent school attendance
- Unsure of the teacher–student role
- Lack of knowledge of school discipline policies
- Lack of knowledge of the critical nature of a high school diploma
- Lack of knowledge of the implications of high-stakes testing

Academic Issues

- Probable interrupted education
- Possibly little or no previous education
- May need basic skills development in math and reading
- Probable gaps in content knowledge from inconsistent schooling
- Possibly limited literacy skills in native language
- Limited knowledge of new school system requirements and expectations

Social Needs Issues

- Lack of proper and adequate clothing and school supplies
- Cultural adjustment assistance
- Need connection to community social services
- Require support for making new friends
- Implications of early marriage for some culture groups
- Implications of living in poverty and high crime areas
- Implications of anti-immigrant attitude (especially if also Muslim)

Mental and Physical Health Issues

- Individual or family counseling may be needed for grief counseling
- Possible victim of violence

- Changes in family roles
- Personal hygiene
- Hearing, dental, and vision screenings
- Vaccinations and medical visit follow-ups
- Consequences of female circumcision for some cultures
- Rare/tropical diseases possible
- Tuberculosis screening and medication
- Posttraumatic stress counseling
- Conflict resolution training

(Bashir-Ali & Custodio, 2002)

Activity: Look through the list of challenges for some refugee students and list how many you may have seen manifest in the past. What supports do your school or school district have to help refugee children adjust to their new life?

The list above is extensive and many of these areas are not typically addressed on a regular basis by local schools or school districts. Working with refugee children and their families can be time-consuming and may require a support system that goes beyond the school walls. Suggestions for both academic and nonacademic assistance will be the focus of the final chapter in this book. Some of the basic requirements will include the following:

- Developmentally appropriate curriculum/materials (basic skills courses for low literacy students and sheltered classes for those with gaps)
- Trained personnel (classroom and support staff) including secretaries, intake personnel, school counselors, school nurses, social workers, administrators
- Expanded learning opportunities to provide additional time for academic growth
- Bilingual personnel to support families and to serve as a bridge to community

Exemplary Support Programs for Refugee Children and Youth

Settlement Workers in Schools

Areas in Canada with large refugee resettlement populations assist in the transition process through an organization called Settlement Workers in Schools or **SWIS**. The Settlement Workers in Schools Program is funded nationally by Immigration, Refugees and Citizenship Canada (IRCC).

The SWIS program places settlement workers from community agencies in elementary and secondary schools that have high numbers of newcomer students. These settlement workers provide information and training to school staffs on the cultures of the students, and serve as a liaison with the parents and the community. Often they bring the parents into the school for workshops on school expectations and connect families with local social services. Additional information on this important program can be found at settlementatwork.org.

On Point to College

Founded in 1999 by Ginny Donahue in Syracuse, New York, this organization assists youth in the transition from high school to college. Their focus is on students who would traditionally struggle with the college entrance process:

- First generation college students (about 90% of their clients)
- Low-income families
- High school graduates or GED recipients who would traditionally not go directly to college
- Young adults who are homeless, aging out of foster care, and refugees
- Adults in recovery or involved in the justice system

Among their 5,800 clients are five who were former "Lost Boys," who have since completed college and returned to South Sudan to help open schools and clinics. One young man, John Dau, was featured in the movie *The Gods Grew Tired of Us*. A number of success stories are featured on the organization website, onpointforcollege.org.

Trauma and Refugee Children

Unlike the difficulty obtaining an exact numbers of refugees with interrupted education and data on its specific effect on students, much research has been done on the impact of trauma on children. While most of the research may not have specifically focused on the unique situations of refugees, the manifestations on behavior in children in general is well documented. It has been shown that chronic exposure to traumatic events, especially during a child's early years, can adversely affect attention, memory, and cognition; reduce a child's ability to focus, organize, and process information; interfere with effective problem solving and or planning, and result in overwhelming feelings of frustration and anxiety. "The situation for adolescent refugees is especially poignant, because they have experienced traumatic events that may affect their general cognitive, social, and sometimes even physical development" (Mace-Matluck, Alexander-Kasparik, & Queen, 1998, p. 12).

Here is how trauma can affect a child's school performance:

- Lower GPA
- Higher rate of absence
- Increased dropout tendency
- More suspensions and expulsions
- Decreased reading ability

Trauma can affect the physical and emotion health of a child. Here are some examples:

- Headaches, stomachaches
- Poor control of emotions
- Inconsistent academic performance
- Unpredictable and or impulsive behavior
- Depression and even suicidal thoughts
- Over- or underreacting to bells, physical contact, doors slamming, sirens, lighting, sudden movements
- Intense reactions to reminders of traumatic events
  ○ Thinking others are watching them
  ○ Blowing up over small situations
  ○ Discomfort with authority figures
  ○ Using violence as a way to solve issues
  ○ Fear of change

It is not difficult to imagine the many situations that may result in trauma for refugee children. People do not become refugees unless some devastating event has occurred that has so interrupted normal life that the only option is flight. In addition to the forced loss of one's home and country, there are often other traumatic events that accompany this journey:

- Death or loss of loved ones
- Witnessing violent acts
- Facing life-threatening situations
- Living in a chaotic or dangerous environment
- Witnessing or being subjected to physical or sexual abuse

What can educators do to help a traumatized child?

- Maintain routines
- Give choices when possible (feeling of power)

- Increase level of support and encouragement
- Have a designated adult for sharing
- Recognize that behavior problems may be a reaction to stimuli
- Be sensitive to the cues that may trigger issues
- Help other students gain sensitivity as well
- When necessary, create a **Section 504** Plan or a plan with similar modifications and accommodations to help manage student trauma.

This information and other helpful suggestions are available on the website nctsn.org. The National Center for Child Traumatic Stress has created a *Child Trauma Toolkit for Educators* (2008) available for download.

Mental Health Support for Refugee Children

At times, the trauma and traumatic events that refugees have faced, and at times continue to face, may be beyond the support that a classroom teacher or even school health professional may be able to provide.

> Many things about the immigrant experience are stressful for children. They are often separated from family for extended periods of time. Some children come from rural or farming communities and are ill equipped to cope with urban settings: others come from refugee camps, after witnessing or experiencing wartime atrocities or person or family violence. Many suffer from post-traumatic stress disorder. ("Children of Immigrants and Refugees," 2011, p. 2)

While the issues and behaviors that may indicate trauma-related problems may first manifest themselves in the classroom, when the teacher sees that the situation requires a response that is beyond the classroom level, the school nurse or psychologist will need to be contacted. So, what is the role of the teacher and when do other professionals need to be involved? We suggest that teachers discuss with the school nurse, the building administrators, school social workers, and any other school personnel such as the school psychologist what the procedures are for working with children who manifest signs of trauma. We also suggest that, if possible, members of the refugee community provide insider information on what the conditions were like in the camps and what family and community issues may be impacting student learning.

What are some of the more extreme signs that intervention may be necessary? The list below was taken from an organization (NetCare) that provides services for children and adults in the Columbus, Ohio, area.

- Preoccupation with violence
- Making violent threats
- Having easy access to weapons
- Use of violence as problem-solving technique when frustrated
- Difficulty with verbal articulation or expression
- Overactive or impulsive behaviors
- Extreme mood swings
- Academic failure
- Low self-esteem or feelings of losing control
- Depression with an attitude that "no one can help me"
- Alienation, rebelliousness, and a lack of social bonding

Except in extreme situations, it is still critical that instruction and routines continue as much as possible. In a study conducted by the Robert Wood Johnson Foundation, the role of the ESL teacher was found to be invaluable.

> ESL classes are perhaps the best known and best used service or program in many of the communities we visited. This study also found that the ESL instructor is one of a few highly trusted individuals that immigrants and refugees turn to for help. "It's the ESL instructors they feel comfortable with, not the regular teachers." (*Living in America*, 2006, p. 23)

While waiting for intervention by other professionals, what should be the role of the ESL and classroom teacher?

> Should teachers probe about traumatic content? While it can be helpful for children to tell their stories, it is not useful to probe about traumatic events. At the same time, children do like to be asked about themselves, about their culture, and about where they came from. It is important not to fall into the other extreme and never ask a child anything about his or her background and past. It is most helpful for teachers to let children know that you are interested in the cultures and countries they have come from, and invite them to share what they would like you and their classmates to know. (Birman, 2012, p. 13)

Even after consulting with mental health professionals, both inside and outside the school environment, some families will refuse services. Some cultures are not familiar with or comfortable with counseling or other outside services. There may not be counselors who speak the language and know the culture of the family, and there may be a strong stigma attached to mental health services. For these families, services provided within the school building may be the best or even only alternative ("Children of Immigrants and Refugees," 2011).

BASIC INFORMATION ON TOP REFUGEE GROUPS IN THE UNITED STATES

From Asia—40% of Total Refugee Population

Bhutan/Nepal

Historical background: The story of the Nepali-speaking Bhutanese refugees begins in the mid- and late 1800s. Large numbers of people from Nepal settled in southern Bhutan during that time and remained in the area peacefully for about 100 years. The Nepali migrants retained their language, Hindu religion, and rural way of life and stayed basically separate from the Buddhist Bhutanese. Then in the 1980s, the mood in the host country changed, and the king of Bhutan and the political leaders of the country decided to remove these Lhotsampas (people of the south). This change was triggered by a combination of factors: fear of the increasingly large Nepali-speaking population, a push by the Nepalis for a more democratic government, and a desire to Bhutanize the country (clear out all non-ethnic Bhutanese). A series of laws were passed, forcing the ethnic Nepalis out of Bhutan. Some fled to India, but most attempted to return to Nepal where they were not greeted with open arms. Forced to live in hastily constructed refugee camps, 100,000 Bhutanese-Nepali lived in these camps for about 20 years, until finally being resettled beginning in 2007 (*Bhutanese Refugees in Nepal,* 2007).

Strengths of the Nepali-Speaking Bhutanese Community

1. About 35% of the refugees speak a "functional" level of English.

2. Because many of the refugees from Bhutan were educated, they attempted to build and run schools for the children, teaching in both Nepali and English.

3. Some of the refugees have been able to leave the camps for study at the university.

4. Family ties are strong and there is a strong sense of community.

5. Although their departure was often hasty and some levels of violence occurred, most families are intact.

Challenges for the Nepali-Speaking Bhutanese Community

1. Very few Nepalis lived in the United States before the resettlement, other than some university students, so there were no large established communities to aid in resettlement.

2. Most of the families had lived in rural areas and were not equipped for urban life.

3. Most families live in multi-generational households and were uncomfortable in a typical U.S. apartment.

4. Most Nepalis have lived under the caste system and bring some of their preconceived ideas with them.

5. Gender roles are distinct and may affect a woman's ability to receive equal opportunities for education and employment.

Burma/Myanmar

Historical background: Refugees from Myanmar (formerly known as Burma) constitute a number of individual tribes who have varied histories, cultures, and languages. The main ethnic group, which lives mainly in the center of the country, is called the Burman and they speak Burmese. The smaller ethnic groups, who live mainly in the hill areas surrounding the central plain, are known by their tribal names and speak languages that are often unintelligible to the other groups. Due to decades of repressive rule, it is these hill tribes who have fled to nearby countries for refuge and who are being resettled. The largest resettlement has been of the Karen, the Karenni, and the Chin people. Each has a distinct language and somewhat distinct culture. Names can be confusing, as each syllable is a separate part of the name and not divided into given and family names. (Compare to Native Americans names such as Running Bear.) Each family member has a distinct two- or three-part name. About 70% of the people from the hill tribes are Buddhist and about 30% Christian (*Refugees from Burma*, 2007).

Strengths of the Burmese Refugee Communities

1. Most groups choose to live near each other, under the leadership of a strong community leader.

2. Strong family ties remain central to each of the culture groups.

3. There is a high value placed on education.

Challenges for the Burmese Refugee Communities

1. The hill tribes lived primarily as farmers, and only a small percentage have skills or trades or are familiar with urban life.

2. Many of the tribes practice traditional medical practices, including cupping and coining, which may appear alarming to Westerners.

3. Because of the history of civil conflict, refugees from the hill tribes distrust ethnic Burmese and prefer to avoid using them as translators or caseworkers. They often cannot communicate with Burmese speakers.

From Africa—25% of Total Refugee Population

Congo (Democratic Republic)

Historical background: The conflict in the Democratic Republic of the Congo (DRC) began in 1996, when many of the perpetrators of the violence and genocide in Rwanda fled to the DRC to regroup and plan a return. Rwanda followed the army into the Congo and 16 years of armed conflict involving many of the surrounding countries led to over 2 million refugees, internally displaced and/or forced into neighboring lands of Rwanda, Uganda, Tanzania, and Burundi. Violence in the area is so prevalent that some civil rights groups have declared the area the most dangerous place in the world to be a woman. The camps are overcrowded and schooling beyond the primary grades is scarce. Very few opportunities for employment or training are available. More than two-thirds of the refugees are younger than 25, with the majority of the families having a single parent or being led by an older sibling. The majority of Congolese refugees are Protestant Christians and have ties to some established religion. About 4% are Muslim. (*Refugees from the Democratic Republic of the Congo,* 2013)

Strengths of the Congolese Community

1. The literacy rate of the adults in the community is about 80%, relatively high for African refugees.

2. Even though these refugees have experienced extreme hardship, they exhibit a strong desire for an education and for employment.

3. The resilience of this population is evident in their ability to remain positive despite their sometimes desperate circumstances.

4. Most Congolese are familiar with Western medicine, but may also practice some traditional healing measures.

Challenges for the Congolese Community

1. Because of the widespread violence in the area, both in the Congo and in the camps, many refugees will have experienced some form of trauma.

2. Mental health practices are virtually unknown and may cause discomfort.

3. Girls tend to marry as young as 14 and boys between 16 and 18.

4. Most Congolese have some exposure to urban life and modern amenities.

Eritrea/Ethiopia

Historical background: In 1952, the UN established the northern portion of Ethiopia, Eritrea, as an independent territory. However, Ethiopia did not recognize this designation and attempted to regain control of the region in the 1960s. A 30-year civil war followed, which resulted in hundreds of thousands of people dead, victims of starvation, internally displaced, or forced to flee as refugees.

Strengths of the Ethiopian/Eritrean Communities

1. Other than the ongoing border dispute, the various ethnic and religious groups in Ethiopia and Eritrea are usually tolerant and accepting of their differences.

2. Most of the refugees are literate and some have a strong educational background.

3. Most are familiar with Western society and often have a trade or skill.

Challenges of the Ethiopian/Eritrean Communities

1. Because of the long-standing violence between Ethiopia and Eritrea, individuals from the two countries may not get along.

2. There are four main languages (Amharic, Tigrinya, Oromo, and Somali) as well as four major religious groups (Muslim, Orthodox or Coptic Christians, Roman Catholics, and Protestants), which can lead to confusion and division.

3. Due to the many years of civil war, many of the refugees have been displaced and homeless for extended periods of time.

4. One people group, the Kunama, have been caught between the two warring countries and are in the process of being resettled in the United States with nowhere else to go.

Somalia

Historical background: Most Somalis left their home country after the clan fighting that led to a civil war that began in 1991, and in some areas continues to disrupt life. The majority of the individuals fled to neighboring Kenya, but some chose to flee to other neighboring Arabic countries such as Yemen and Saudi Arabia. After several years in refugee camps, Somalis began to be resettled in third countries in the late 1990s.

Strengths of the Somali Community

1. Strong sense of Somali identity

2. Resistance to racism

3. Positive attitude toward education

4. Strong sense of community

5. Desire to be involved in education of children

Challenges for Somali Community

1. Many children and adults have limited educational backgrounds and high rates of illiteracy, especially women and those who lived in rural areas

2. Lack of resources

3. Parenting challenges

4. Generation gap

5. Fear of losing "Somaliness" or home culture

6. Attitude toward Islam by some Americans

Tips for teachers: Minneapolis has the largest number of Somalis in the United States, and the Minneapolis Public Schools' website has a number of documents for educators who work with Somali students.

Somali Bantus

Historical background: The Bantu are a minority group who lived in the southern part of Somalia known as "between the rivers," which was the major agricultural region of the country. Most of the Bantu came to Somalia in the early 1800s, some voluntarily to work and others came as slaves. Many converted to Islam after arriving, possibly to escape slavery because no Muslim may own another Muslim. The Bantu for the most part were treated as second-class citizens, were undereducated, and not permitted to hold positions of power. Their poor treatment after arrival in the refugee camps resulted in them receiving preferential resettlement opportunities, and almost 12,000 Somali Bantus left the Kenyan camps in the mid- and late 2000s.

Strengths of the Bantu Community

1. Strong sense of community, willing to help each other

2. Usually peaceful and appreciative of friendship and assistance

3. Willing to accept temporary manual labor positions and eager to better themselves

4. Enjoy community events with music and dancing

Challenges of the Bantu Community

1. Most Bantu adults have little or no education.

2. They often live in isolated communities with little ties to outside.

3. As with ethnic Somalis, the war has left many families with a single female parent.

4. While most Bantu men were farmers in Somalia, they are being resettled in predominately urban settings with few marketable skills.

5. Some Bantu bring their traditional medicinal practices with them, and this may lead to conflicts with modern medicine.

Sudan/South Sudan

Historical background: Sudan was formed in 1898 by joining eight provinces into one country. Most of the northern provinces had Arabic roots and were followers of Islam, including the capital of Khartoum. The southernmost province, Equitoria, was predominately Christian and agricultural. When Sudan gained its independence in 1958, it was promised that the southern province would be free to follow its previous lifestyle and religion, but this promise was not kept. Two civil wars followed, and in 1987, the armies of the north attacked the southern province, destroying many of the villages. The boys who had been away from the villages with the cattle returned home to find everyone killed, and they fled north to Ethiopia. After walking for months, these children, some as young as 6 or 7, arrived in Ethiopia and became known as the Lost Boys of Sudan.

In 1991, a war broke out in Ethiopia and these young men were forced to run again. About half of the 20,000 children made it to Kenya and began a new phase of their life in Kakuma Refugee Camp. Ten years later, about 3,600 of these former children were resettled in the United States. Peace talks in 2005 led to a shaky period of lessened violence, and a referendum in 2011 formed the free country of South Sudan. Unfortunately, internal political issues and external violence continues to plague the country, and refugees continue to escape, looking for peace in neighboring countries.

Strengths of the Sudanese Community

1. Most of the refugees who have come from Kakuma have a relatively strong educational background, and many have some job skills.

2. English is the official language of South Sudan, and it was used in the schools in Kakuma, so most refugees have at least an intermediate level of proficiency.

3. These refugees, especially the Lost Boys, have a strong sense of community and demonstrate high levels of resilience.

Challenges of the Sudanese Community

1. More recent refugees from the Sudan or South Sudan have lived through almost constant war, famine, and gender violence, needing trauma-related support.

2. The literacy rate in South Sudan is only 27%.

3. Only 5% of the population lives to the age of 55, the median age is 17. Families are often separated.

4. There is still distrust between refugees from the north and the south, and they will probably not work well together.

From the Middle East—35% of the Total Refugee Population

Afghanistan

Historical background: Afghanistan is an ethnically diverse country that has been plagued by political and religious violence for almost 40 years. The first refugees arrived after the Soviet invasion if 1979 and the numbers have been small but somewhat steady until the Iraq war 25 years later. Many of the refugees coming now have faced persecution and even torture at the hands of the Taliban, especially women who have been victimized under this extremist regime. Two-thirds of recent refugees from Afghanistan are children (Robson & Lipson, 2002). (There is discussion of whether Afghanistan should be listed as a Middle-Eastern country or part of South-Central Asia. Under the Bush Administration, it was listed as in the "Greater Middle East," but most other references consider it Asian. It is listed here as part of the Middle East because it is similar in culture and politics to Iraq and Iran.)

Strengths of the Afghan Community

1. Most of the early Afghan refugees were well-educated and had ties to the small Afghan community already living in the United States.

2. Despite the many issues of living in a society where extremist Islamic law was followed, the strict adherence to the Quran philosophy of respect for women sometimes has the advantage of providing safely and security in a country at war.

3. Family ties are strong and can provide support during the initial transition period.

Challenges for the Afghan Community

1. Life if Afghanistan changed dramatically after the Russian invasion, and most of the challenges faced by Afghan refugees are directly or indirectly a result of this:

   a. Public education had always been rare, and after the invasion, most Afghans obtained schooling only in religious settings, and it was only for boys.

   b. Women were not permitted to have any public life, and sometimes when women arrive in the United States, they are still afraid to report domestic violence or educational neglect.

   c. Islamic law dominated society, and life in Western countries will demand adjustments.

2. The political and ethnic divisions found in Afghanistan often carry over to the new communities.

Iran

Historical background: The history of Iranian immigration to the United States is very different from most of the other countries discussed in this chapter. Most of the Iranian-born immigrants in the United States came as students or through more typical immigrant channels such as work or family reunification. Another large group came under a temporary visa and then requested asylum. Some of these asylum requests date back to the fall of the Shah in 1979, but many are within the last 10 years. Another unique situation of Iran is that there are hundreds of thousands of Afghan and Iraqi refugees fleeing into the country, while native Iranians are leaving and requesting refugee status as they leave the country. Many of those leaving are political dissidents or religious minorities fearing reprisals by the extremist leadership in Iran.

Strengths of the Iranian Community

1. With almost 300,000 Iranians living in the United States, there are several strong communities established to support new arrivals.

2. Most Iranians are very well educated and represent the educational elite of the country, causing what is termed a "brain drain" in Iran.

3. Since many of the new arrivals are leaving Iran under tourist visas or to reunite with family members, they are coming with resources to start businesses or set up households independently.

Challenges for the Iranian Community

1. Despite being educated and having professional positions in Iran, the new arrivals are often finding it difficult to transition to equivalent positions in the United States due to language or licensing issues.

2. With large Iranian communities already established, the immigrants may not see the necessity to integrate into the larger American society.

3. Despite the geographic and religious ties to other Middle Eastern countries, the history and language of Iran are distinct and may prevent mingling with Arabic-speaking refugees.

Iraq

Historical background: Most Iraqis are being displaced due to issues resulting from the Iraq War, which began in 2002. There has traditionally been unrest and distrust between the two major Muslim groups in Iraq (the Sunnis and the Shiites), and also amongst the many ethnic and religious minorities in the country, including the Kurds, the Baha'is, the Chaldeans, the Jews, and Yazidis. Saddam Hussein's Ba'ath party kept the unrest in check with his repressive measures, but with his departure, the violence has increased exponentially. Many of the Iraqis had fled to neighboring Syria, only to be caught up in the political and religious struggle there. Resettlement into a third country is being recommended by the UNHCR, but with the Syrian crisis taking the forefront, the fate of the Iraqi refugees is unclear.

Strengths of the Iraqi Community

1. Most of the Iraqi refugees have a strong education, and many were professionals before being displaced.

2. Most Iraqis have lived in urban areas with modern conveniences and adjust well with urban resettlement.

3. Woman in Iraq had much more freedom than women in many other Middle Eastern countries and adapt to life in Western countries relatively easily.

Challenges of the Iraqi Community

1. Many of the well-educated Iraqi refugees have problems obtaining equivalent employment due to language or certification barriers and may arrive with unrealistic expectations of finding employment quickly.

2. Because of the extended war and displacement, many Iraqi refugees are dealing with posttraumatic stress.

3. Even though Iraq was less orthodox than many Muslim countries in the Middle East, there was still a strong separation of genders, which may lead to discomfort in social situations in the United States.

Syria

Historical background: For the past 40 years, Syria has been ruled by the Ba'ath party: the same political organization that supported Saddam Hussein in Iraq. When the Arab Spring uprisings of 2011 swept the Middle East, protests against the government of Syria led to violent reprisals. Over time, various other groups became involved in the conflict, including extremists from northern Iraq (ISIS and ISIL), Russia, and NATO-aligned countries including the United States. It is estimated that about half the country (as many as 10 million) is either internally displaced or has fled to other countries for refuge. The pressure of overcrowding on the neighboring countries of Turkey, Lebanon, and Jordan has led to hundreds of thousands fleeing into Europe for safety. Fear that terrorists may use the cover of these refugees to infiltrate into receiving countries has sparked international debates on the resettlement of Syrian refugees. (At the time of the writing of this book, the situation in Syria is dire and in a constant state of flux. We have tried to put information that is as current as possible, but it may have changed by the time you read this book.)

Strengths of Syrian Community

1. Before the 2011 revolt, education in the country was strong, and the literacy rate was 77% for women and over 90% for men.

2. Most Syrians lived in cities with modern amenities, with a large percentage having a secondary school education and many with university credentials.

3. Before the revolt, Syria was known for its religious tolerance and ethnic diversity.

4. Syrians are known for their entrepreneurial spirit and are willing to work hard for their future.

Challenges of the Syrian Community

1. Because of the unrest and widespread violence, schools have closed and most people have been unable to work. Famine and fear have driven half the country from its home. Bombings and roving armies have destroyed most of the country's infrastructure.

2. The neighboring countries of Jordan, Lebanon, and Turkey have no more room for the refugees, and this overcrowding is leading to the crisis in Europe. While the first refugees found homes, education, and health care, the later arrivals were not able to obtain these basic necessities.

3. Although fairly tolerant of diversity, Syrian men and women prefer to work with others of their own gender and will feel uncomfortable if forced to deal with the opposite sex.

Syria has become the defining humanitarian challenge of our time. . . .
Providing refuge for vulnerable people fleeing war is of life-saving importance for the individuals affected, but it's also an important show of solidarity with countries of the region that are hosting millions of Syrians.
("Governments Pledge," 2014)

For additional information about the history of each of the groups listed above, the background on the conflicts that led to flight, as well as more specifics about issues dealing with resettlement and education, please check out the websites for the Center for Applied Linguistics (cal.org), Bridging Refugee Youth and Children's Services (brycs.org), and the Migration Policy Institute (migrationpolicy.org).

For Further Study

1. What are the benefits to educators of knowing the process of refugee resettlement? What social and religious organizations in your community could be called upon to serve as resources for increasing your school's understanding of your refugee population?

2. There are many myths and misconceptions about how refugees are resettled and what benefits they receive upon arrival. What myths have you heard, and what did you read in this chapter that refutes some of those rumors? How can these rumors affect the attitude and responses of students and staff who interact with refugees?

3. What does your school or school district do to help newly arrived children adjust to their new surroundings?

4. How do the educational opportunities for refugees in the camps impact their readiness for schooling upon arrival in their new country? What specifically can your school or school district do to help ameliorate the lack of a strong educational background for these students?

5. The negative effects of trauma can definitely have an impact on children's learning and relationships. Can you think of a time when a child demonstrated some of the physical or academic manifestations of posttraumatic stress? What school-based resources did you have to support the child in this situation? How could schools be better prepared to assist children who have experienced trauma?

6. Which of the refugee groups listed in this chapter is present in your community? How are your school and your community prepared to assist these children with the challenges of interrupted education and cultural dissonance? When a new cultural group arrives, what steps does or will your school take to learn about their history and culture?

7. After reading this chapter, prepare a short presentation for your school on tips for working with refugee children. What areas do you think are the most important to cover? What community resources do you have that you could offer to the teachers/staff? You could use the following vignettes as an activity.

Vignettes

Review the following student vignettes to highlight the types of issues you may experience when serving refugee children. Think about the background of the child, what he or she may have experienced that could have contributed to their situation, and what academic programming and social services may be needed to help this child thrive.

Aisha is a 12-year-old girl from Afghanistan. She left Afghanistan when she was 8 and fled to Pakistan with her family. She had never gone to school in Afghanistan and had very little opportunity to attend school in the refugee camp. She is barely literate in Pashto, and can only do basic math problems. She clings to another girl in her class and seldom talks. Her sixth-grade teacher is unsure how best to help her feel more safe and comfortable, and ready to participate in classroom activities.

Simon is a 15-year-old from the Democratic Republic of the Congo. He was not even born when the situation in neighboring Rwanda brought violence and disruption to his hometown. He was separated from his mother when he was 11 and does not know if she is still alive. He came to the United States as part of the Unaccompanied Refugee Minor program and has been placed in a foster family. He had about 6 years of schooling between his home country and the camp in Tanzania, and is literate in French.

Dia Wja is a 17-year-old girl from Burma. She is a member of the Karen tribe and has lived in a refugee camp in Thailand for 5 years. Her parents fled Burma because of political upheaval, which resulted in her entire village being destroyed. She was able to attend school only about 2 days a week because she was responsible for the care of her two younger brothers. She wants to obtain a high school diploma but is frustrated at being placed in ninth grade because she had no transcripts from her schooling in the camps. She is extremely shy, and afraid and embarrassed to discuss her situation with her teachers and school counselor.

Omar is a 14-year-old boy from Syria. He has lived with his family in Turkey for 3 years before resettling in Toronto. He had an excellent education until he was 10, when the schools closed and he had to leave his middle-class home. He seems angry and sullen, refusing to participate in most classroom activities.

Nasteho was born in a refugee camp in Kenya, where she lived with her Somali Bantu mother and three siblings until she was 8. She arrived in the United States and was placed in third grade, although she had never been to school. She is now in middle school, but is constantly struggling to catch up to her peers. She has been tested for possible learning problems, but the school psychologist could not determine if her difficulties came from her lack of previous education and decided against special education. Her mother was against the placement and told the school that she would not agree with any decision to place her child in special programming.

4 PROVIDING SOCIAL AND EMOTIONAL SUPPORT

DEVELOPING RESILIENT STUDENTS

Imagine you are a refugee child. Everything has changed in your life. Your grandmother who loved you so much and took care of you isn't with you. Your winter clothes feel heavy and awkward. Everything feels and smells very different. You don't understand what is happening but you sense the tension in your family, especially from your mother.

—Ho (2005, p. 16)

INTRODUCTION

Whether a recent refugee, fleeing persecution due to race, religion, nationality, or as a member of a targeted social and/or political group, or an immigrant, coming to the United States, seeking economic stability, education, employment, or fleeing a natural disaster, English learners sense these acute changes in their lives. They express the stress they are experiencing in a number of ways. Young English learners **(ELs)** may become clingy, cry, and refuse to be separated from a parent or trusted caregiver. Aggressive protective actions may include biting, kicking, and hair pulling, and/or reverting to toddler behaviors, such as thumb sucking.

Stress, whether in response to a traumatic event, crisis, or significant changes in lifestyle, in both young and older learners blocks their ability to learn. The emotional and/or physical traumas experienced by English learners can affect their cognitive, social-emotional, and both first- and second-language development. Additionally, the dramatic impact of migration includes the feeling of isolation, challenges to one's ethnic identity, and often changing family roles and dynamics.

Teachers may find that students are restless, forgetful, demonstrate poor concentration, are easily distracted, or prone to daydreaming. Some ELs may feel abandoned as they try to cope with now living with relatives they may have never previously known after their parents have been deported. Aggressive behaviors, due to frustration and overly sensitive emotions, may include impulsive responses such as fighting with peers, parents, and teachers or other authority figures.

WHAT IS RESILIENCE?

Educators have often wondered how some English learners overcome all the changes and challenges they face and succeed emotionally and educationally, while others do not. Resilience, the ability to become strong, healthy, or successful again after something bad happens, or to recover from and adjust to change, accounts for this difference.

Resilience is the ability to persist and adapt to change and/or adverse circumstances. It is a human attribute that helps students to positively adapt, change behaviors after trauma, and to persevere, even when subsequent obstacles are present. Resilient learners have developed the resources to cope, demonstrated flexibility to adjust to learning challenges, and discovered the ability to recover from learning response errors.

Understanding What ELs Face: Immigrants and Refugees

Early Issues: Culture Shock—Phases 1 and 2

Culture shock affects every person who finds himself or herself living in a new community, whether within his or her own country or another, with unfamiliar customs, social cues, community norms, language, gestures, and general daily practices. For English learners, both SIFE and immigrants, culture shock can result in overwhelming feelings of sadness, anxiety, frustration and fear, living in an unknown place with an incomprehensible language.

Culture shock normally manifests itself in four phases. The first is the honeymoon phase, with a sense of excitement about the new culture. It is a phase that is short-lived, due to information overload and the realization regarding communication and/or understanding the nuances of the new language and culture.

The frustration phase is next, in which there are either attempts to negotiate the new environment or to withdraw. During this phase, students may become fearful to speak or interact with others in the mainstream community, feel lonely and apprehensive of rejection by peers. (See Chapter 3, this volume, and the National Child Traumatic Stress Network for more details at www.nctsn.org/trauma-types/refugee-trauma.)

Some physical and emotional signs of culture shock include the following:

- **Physical symptoms**
  - Frequent illness (e.g., viruses, low-grade infections, coughs, headaches, stomachaches, etc.)
  - Sleepy, listless, insomnia, and feel tired all the time, causing inability to concentrate
  - Nervous habits, such as nail, lip, or finger biting; scratching a site (e.g., arm, nose, etc.), and/or pulling out individual hairs (e.g., eyelashes, eyebrows, or from the head)

- **Emotional symptoms**
  - Anxiety and fears of separation from siblings, parents, or caretakers
  - Regressive behaviors in young children (e.g., bed wetting, wetting clothing at school, thumb sucking, etc.)
  - Volatile behavior or extremely passive behavior
  - Long silent period, selective mutism
  - Thoughts of trauma that will not stop
  - Feelings of helplessness or hopelessness
  - Frustration, extreme sadness, or demonstrating an overly sensitive response to a situation

For these first two stages of culture shock, it is important to work with parents, caregivers, school social workers, and psychologists to develop plans for responses to each type of behavior to help refugee and immigrant children and their families to cope with these challenges and build their resiliency. It is also important for school and community support teams to help teachers understand what they can do to create a safe and welcoming environment in their classrooms.

What can schools and teachers do?

- **Schoolwide Programs**
  Social skills instruction, or social and emotional learning, for all students, whether they are nonnative newcomers or native-born English speakers, helps to build resilience in the entire school

population. Programs built around social skills instruction for all students would include modeling how to express your emotions, appropriate ways to make and keep friendships, how to deal with negative situations in school and the community, as well as how to build an awareness and understanding of the messages sent by body language. Students are also taught to accept and respect differences, including language and cultural differences among their peers.

- **Classroom Applications**
  Social skills instruction extends to all aspects of school, in academic classrooms, on the playground, school bus, and in the gym and sports events. Teachers are prepared to reinforce the schoolwide program learning within their classrooms. Teachers promote a positive environment through creating a community of learners with such things as common rules and expectations of all students, morning meetings to set the tone of the day, and instruction in personal responsibility and collaborative problem solving within the classroom. In addition, classroom teachers or other school personnel, such as the school social worker, can meet with small groups of students during lunchtime to further develop relationships with students and to provide an opportunity for sharing of successes, as well as concerns.

Teachers can helps ELs learn how to deal with the various problems encountered both inside and outside of the classroom that affect learning and social and emotional adjustment. Teachers need to be first aware of the "red flags" in student behavior indicating acute responses to trauma. Addressing an immediate problem requires a different set of strategies in contrast to building a community of resilient learners.

Students needing immediate attention may exhibit one of the following, or other serious behaviors:

- Withdrawn and noncommunicative in any language
- Excessively verbalizing about an event or denying the event ever occurred
- Refusing to follow established school or classroom rules, confrontational language
- Aggressive behavior toward peers, fighting physically or verbally; damaging peer's property
- Extreme sadness or crying without a specific cause

At this point determine if this is an emergency. Speak with the student, without confrontational language. Be sensitive and empathetic. Let your school counselor and/or social worker know immediately. More information for "red flag'" situations can be found at The Safe Start National Resource Center (https://safestartcenter.wordpress.com) and the National Child Traumatic Stress Network (www.nctsn.org).

Another resource for preparing staff and parents, creating a welcoming environment, caring, and guiding behavior, and suggestions for responses to culture shock is www.settlementatwork.org. Although the focus of this document is on Syrian refugee children, there are appropriate applications to other cultures and other arrival situations that can be gleaned. There is an excellent t-chart of possible signs of culture shock and suggested responses for both physical and emotional signs that could become a model for schools to develop their own.

Following is a checklist of teacher actions and attitudes to help ensure that a classroom is adequately supporting SIFE.

What can I do to support my students with interrupted education?

- I will begin each lesson by activating prior knowledge and/or building background for all topics/lessons.
- I have and will continue to provide an environment of print in the classroom.
- I will engage the students in hands-on learning.
- I will limit the amount of new vocabulary each day.
- I will check for comprehension frequently, not with just "Do you understand?".
- My assessments will accurately provide opportunities to show understanding.
- I will regularly allow students to work in groups.
- I will integrate the native language and culture whenever possible.
- I will incorporate both language and content objectives in each lesson and refer to them throughout the lesson. Both my students and I will self-assess when objectives have been met.
- My expectations are and will always be realistic yet rigorous.

Ongoing: Language, Communication, Acculturation

Culture Shock—Phases 3 and 4

Within the first year, English learners begin to "adjust" (Phase 3) to the new culture and begin to learn the new/second language for social interaction and to learn some **academic language** needed for academic schoolwork. There are still many ongoing experiences in which there is a mismatch of cultural responses to peers, teachers, and others in the community. These may include gestures, body language proxemics, eye contact, and language usage, and register.

When students reach the adaption stage (Phase 4) they are able to participate fully in the culture, feel comfortable speaking the second language for both academic and social purposes, with few errors and with an expanded vocabulary. They have acculturated, able to use both their native language and their new language for communicative purposes. They have internalized how and when to appropriately respond to cultural cues in both languages and cultures. Neither culture nor language is considered inferior to the other. Both are valued for the communicative resources the languages offer to support the student as a bilingual bicultural child.

(Note: In Chapter 5, this volume, we offer programming suggestions and instructional models for students.)

THREE APPROACHES TO BUILDING RESILIENCE

In Chapter 3, we discussed and listed the social and academic needs of newly arrived refugees with interrupted education. While this list is linked specifically to refugees, it also applies to other students with interrupted formal education. Building a classroom and school community of resilient learners can be accomplished through the incorporation of various strategies. Researched approaches to building resilient students, to be described and discussed below, include:

- "I Have, I Am, I Can," (Davis, 2013/2014; Grotberg, 1995)
- Reading and Writing Migration Narratives (Stewart, 2015)
- "Havens of Resilience: The Resiliency Wheel" (Henderson, 2013)

I Have, I Am, I Can

In *A Guide to Promoting Resilience in Children: Strengthening the Human Spirit,* Grotberg (1995) introduced three key instructional strategies for developing resilience, which she labeled "I Have, I Am, and I Can." As important as teaching content and facilitating the learning of academic language across the curriculum, with the "I Have" strategy, teachers help students understand the resources and supports that are available to them and for their families. Understanding these resources and how to access them provides a sense of security and helps students be "available" to learning. It also helps teachers connect to their students, as more than educators, but as people interested in the whole child.

Grotberg states that the "I Have" resilience resources sends the message that I have people around me who care about me; they will model appropriate behavior; and they want me to learn and do things on my own, but are here to support me, and will help me when I am sick, in a difficult situation, or need help learning. It is important for educators to be one of the "I Have's," and to be available to listen to and support students.

Reaching out to students and their parents to provide the "I Have" can have obstacles. With EL parents, there is always the language barrier and trust. It is also critical to find translators and community members who speak the same language, as well as providing a list of resources, in the native language or in simple English. Additionally, family workshops in school will provide them with information about the supports available in school and in the community.

Explaining resilience to nonnative EL parents can be quite difficult. Resilience, as Grotberg (1995) indicates, does not translate easily into other languages. The term and concepts involved with overcoming adversity and acculturating to a new life are not easily explained or modeled. Grotberg indicates that "the vocabulary of resilience is more than a set of words . . . it is a set of tools" (p. 8). Learning the language of resilience, the vocabulary needed to "reinforce feelings and beliefs" about becoming resilient, both students and their parents can "recognize resilience in themselves" and create the "I Have."

Grotberg has indicated that supporting resilience in children should start early. Parents need to support infants and toddlers by expressing love, acknowledging a child's feelings and fears. They need to encourage children to see and understand what he or she has (the "I Have") so that parents would model confidence in the now and optimism for the future.

Outward expressions of love and discussions of feelings and fears are not in the cultural norms of some newcomer populations. Parents will need to be helped to understand the importance of open communication with their children in building self-confidence and minimizing and/or eliminating fears, manifested in the physical and emotional symptoms described earlier in this chapter.

It is important that parent–teacher interactions emphasize the positives, rather than noting the language and learning deficits in parent–teacher conferences or Back-to-School Nights. Creating a connection and opening lines of communication and trust only happen when teachers approach parents with the possibilities for learning, not the deficits the newcomer has at this moment in time. Teachers can also be a resource for parents in connecting to school services and community resources. Learning the language of resilience, the vocabulary needed to "reinforce feelings and beliefs" about becoming resilient, both students and their parents can "recognize resilience in themselves" and create the "I Have."

Figure 4.1 Sample "I Have" Worksheet

Family Support	School Supports	Community Supports
Parent(s)	English teacher	Church, synagogue, or mosque
Older sibling	School counselor School nurse	Health clinic
Grandparent(s)	Classmate	Cultural group

With the second strategy, "I Am," English learners use the power of the narrative to tell their stories. Who am I? Why am I here? What have I learned? What will I learn next? Daily journal writing has been supported in research (Pennebaker, 1997; Pennebaker & Smyth, 2016) as having "therapeutic power." Daily journal free writes can provide teachers with insights into the English learner's movement toward becoming a resilient student. The anonymity of the writer can also provide the teacher with insights about the student into concerns, fears, questions, as well as both feelings of frustration and, conversely, feelings about accomplishments.

Since "I Am" journals are very personal and provide an outlet for expressing what cannot often be expressed in words, English learners need to be assured of the confidentiality of the content shared with teachers. Additionally, teachers need to discuss with students whether they wish to have a one-way (teachers can read, but do not respond) or two-way journal (teachers respond to posts). Teachers never correct grammar or language in the journal. ELs can write in English and/or native language or combinations of both.

The power of the journal provides students with a vehicle to pour ideas onto paper without concern about writing conventions, organization of ideas, grammar, or spelling. They can privately choose to share or not with a teacher their struggles, questions, and/or successful moments leading up to becoming resilient. An additional benefit of the journal is to help develop English-language skills, build prosody and fluency.

"I Can," the third strategy, connects "I Have" and "I Am" through the use of a problem-based model for both socio-cultural and academic learning. Within the socio-cultural realm, English learners are able to utilize their "I Have" and "I Am" and be helped to negotiate solutions to problems, communicate both problem-solving strategies, share personal viewpoints, and manage emotions. Throughout "I Can" socio-cultural learning situations, and with the help of teachers, English learners discover ways to share feelings and concerns, discuss conflicts and learn ways to solve problems. They learn how to seek out others with whom they can comfortably communicate.

Figure 4.2 What I Can Do Now and What I Will Do Soon

"I Can Do Now"	"I Will Be Able to Do Soon"	Steps to Take
Request help with reading when I don't understand.	Complete my homework on time.	

Edutopia author Rebecca Alber suggests, in her online blog/article (June 1, 2016) "3 End-of-Year Reflection Strategies for Students," that students could craft a letter to their future selves. In this letter students could report memories of things learned this past year (the "I Can Do Now") and record their hopes, fears, and expectations for the upcoming school year (the "I Will Be Able to Do Soon"). Although students would or could indicate their fears for the upcoming year, a less negative word such as "concerns" or "worries" about the future would encourage a more positive approach, than the use of the word "fears." English learners should be looking forward to adding to the "I Will Be Able to Do Soon" list and focusing on how they are becoming resilient learners, including ways to address their worries.

In the area of teaching and learning, problem-centered/problem-based models of instruction empower the students to use the "I Can" strategy to demonstrate their learning. Organizing content into a problem-centered inquiry, where students interact with the learning materials, learning across the curriculum, and working cooperatively with others, provides opportunities for students to not only develop academic language, but also to use their socio-cultural problem-solving skills at an academic level and conversely academic problem solving in life situations.

Janine S. Davis (2013/2014), in "Building Resilient Students: Three Strategies for Success," mentions two models for problem-centered teaching, which would not only build concept knowledge, but also provide a model for developing persistence and becoming resilient learners. The first model, an inquiry chart, would consist of a series of questions about an instructional problem (and could be used with a social or cultural issue). The students would collaboratively look for and determine resources, which might provide answers. The students, guided by the teacher, would work together to find solutions and determine a course of action related to the original question. Davis indicates that the process of research and inquiry, although not a clear course of action, nor an easily discovered endpoint, provides students with experiences in learning to persist and become resilient.

Figure 4.3 I Have, I Am, I Can Venn Diagram

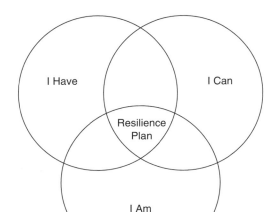

Reading and Writing Migration Narratives

Expanding on the "I Am," educators can validate student migration experiences and connect reading, class discussion, and journaling; teachers can carefully choose specific themed literature as prompts. Migration stories and particularly well-crafted **picture books** can provide students with opportunities for reflection and expression on their own migration story. In a recent *Journal of Adolescent and Adult Literacy*, A. Stewart (2015) in "My Journey of Hope and Peace" describes an instructional unit the author developed to teach adolescent refugees reading and writing built around the use of migration stories. Using three key migration nonfiction books, two picture books, and one wordless book; students created the narrative (for the wordless book), and then read aloud or did shared reading and class discussion connected to their own migration stories. Students wrote journal entries, created illustrations, and even created a comic strip to tell their stories. Journaling expanded beyond Stewart's expectation as students wrote about their pre-refugee lives, their reasons for coming to America, and the challenges they endured.

Migration narratives provide for a rich teaching and learning experience. Students are provided with opportunities to show teachers their funds of knowledge. Writing their own stories validates their experiences and empowers students to define their individuality. Literacy skills are modeled through text examples, and students increase their academic vocabularies, and learn to write from reading and discussions of modeled texts.

Table 4.1 Recommended Resources for Migration Stories and Biographies

Books
Asgedom, M. (2004). *Of Beetles and Angels: A Boy's Remarkable Journey From a Refugee Camp to Harvard.* Chicago, IL: Mawi, Inc. An autobiographical account of a family from Ethiopia that relocates to Chicago as refugees.
Beah, I. (2008). *A Long Way Gone: Memoirs of a Boy Soldier.* New York, NY: Sarah Crichton Books at Farrar, Straus, and Giroux. The true story of a teen who was forced into a paramilitary group in Sierra Leone and his eventual escape and rehabilitation.
Bode, J. (1989). *New Kids in Town: Oral History of Immigrant Teens.* New York, NY: Scholastic. Interviews of 13 teens describing their immigration stories.
Jiminez, F. (1997). *The Circuit: Stories From the Life of a Migrant Child.* University of New Mexico Press. Autobiography of Francisco Jiminez's life as the son of a migrant worker. Others in the series, and good reads as the author describes how he moves from migrant child to university professor, include *Breaking Through* (2002), *Reaching Out* (2009), and *Taking Hold* (2015).
Mead, A. (2003). *Year of No Rain.* New York, NY: Farrar, Straus, and Giroux. A fictionalized account of the story of the Lost Boys of Sudan.
Nazario, S. (2014). *Enrique's Journey (the young adult adaptation): The True Story of a Boy Determined to Reunite With His Mother.* New York, NY: Ember Books. Description of the journey many Central American teens make to come to the United States.
Van Wyk, C. (2009). *Long Walk to Freedom.* Illustrated Children's Edition. London, UK: Macmillan Children's Books. Picture book version of Mandela's official autobiography of the same name.
Yousafzai, M. (2016). *I Am Malala: How One Girl Stood Up for Education and Changed the World* [Young Readers Edition]. New York, NY: Little, Brown Books for Young Readers. Autobiographical account of a girl from Pakistan who was shot by the Taliban for attending school. Several picture book versions of Malala's story are also available.
Videos
He Named Me Malala (https://www.amazon.com/s/ref=nb_sb_ss_i_1_8?url=search-alias%3Dmovies-tv&field-keywords=he+named+me+malala&sprefix=He+named%2Cmovies-tv%2C197)
I Learn America (http://ilearnamerica.com)
Live and Become (https://www.amazon.com/Live-Become-Yael-Abecassis/dp/B0011ZJ5BS)
Lost Boys of Sudan (https://www.amazon.com/s/ref=nb_sb_noss_2?url=search-alias%3Dmovies-tv&field-keywords=Lost+Boys+of+Sudan&rh=n%3A2625373011%2Ck%3ALost+Boys+of+Sudan)

"Havens of Resilience"

Nan Henderson in "Havens of Resilience" (2013) indicates that "schools are natural environments for helping all children cultivate the resilience that resides within them" (p. 22). She suggests that the power of resilience is based on both a student's internal and external environmental protective factors. Henderson's **resiliency wheel,** based on a body of resilience research, connects both "caring and support" to the conditions present in classrooms to support growth for all students. She indicates that school climate, developed through teacher–student relationships was "the most powerful factor" in the development of resilient learners. For Henderson, the key elements of school climate, as modeled on the resiliency wheel include the following:

- Staff and students know that they are in a safe place
- Teacher–students creating supportive relationships
- Students being viewed as valued members and resources in the school community, through engagement and empowerment
- Students knowing that there are clear rules and boundaries within the classroom and across the school
- Students are being awareness of the school's high expectations for their academic performance and appropriate school and classroom behavior
- Staff and students sharing a philosophy of trust, respect, and a philosophy of caring

How can educators of English learners use this resiliency wheel to focus on their specific needs in the classroom and school? With the overarching theme of "caring and support," which Henderson considers "the single most powerful environmental protective factor," the resiliency wheel can be used by all school personnel, working together, to develop and implement a schoolwide plan.

In the area of academics and instruction, individual schools and school districts need to develop models for and to share consistent messages concerning student and teacher expectations of performance. "Schools," as Henderson (2013) indicates, "are natural environments for helping all children cultivate the resilience that resides within them" (p. 22).

Figure 4.4 "Social and Emotional" Whole School Climate Diagram

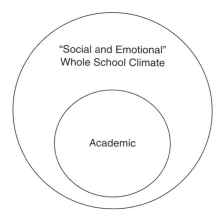

Table 4.2 School Climate Components

- **Social and emotional:** Key Ideas (What is needed to set the tone for resilience in order to grow and succeed?)
  - ○ School is viewed as a safe and welcoming place for both ELs and their parents.
  - ○ Students are viewed as assets to the school community, creating a mosaic of cultures represented.
  - ○ Students and parents are made aware that the school is a caring environment, where ELs are respected and encouraged to openly share their language and culture.

- **Social and emotional:** Creating the Plan
  - ○ Ongoing professional development for all instructional personnel regarding cultural differences, learning, and language challenges
  - ○ Outreach in the community for community members to serve as parent supports, translators, etc.
  - ○ Sensitivity training, including learning about the cultural differences of the ELs and their families, for all noninstructional staff, such as school secretaries, school nurses, lunchroom aides, bus drivers, truant officers, etc.
  - ○ School environment visually demonstrates that all cultures are welcome—school décor and artifacts. The various cultures of the school are visible when entering the school, thus representing the school as a multicultural community of learners.

- **Academic:** School and Districtwide Guidelines
  - ○ Expectations and Boundaries—Provide clear and consistent schoolwide classroom academic expectations and behavioral boundaries.
  - ○ Provide consistent and ongoing opportunities for all students to participate in meaningful classroom instructional and social interactions.
  - ○ Teach both academics and life skills.

For Further Study

1. Research community and school resources in your area. Create an "I Have" list of resources that could be used to help the students in your setting. Develop a list specific to your context and to parents, students, and other educators in your setting.

2. Check out the following resources on social and emotional learning:

    - Responsive Classroom Approach: www.responsiveclassroom.org/about/principles-practices/

    - Collaborative for Academic, Social, and Emotional Learning: www.casel.org

    - The National Child Traumatic Stress Network: Refugee Trauma: www.nctsn.org/trauma-types/refugee-trauma

    - Care for Newcomer Children: Supporting the Care and Settlement for Young Immigrant Children: http://cmascanada.ca The website is based in Canada but includes many refugee resources, including TEDtalk videos about refugees, World Refugee Day, and a report on the educational experiences of refugee children.

3. Create Personal Journals: How could you use dialogue journals to support the English learners in your setting? What ways would you use to model this "I Am" strategy for colleagues and encourage their use throughout the curriculum?

4. "I Can" Ethnobiography: How could ELs model their social and cultural strengths through this writing model?

    a. Which literature would you choose for a reading component?

    b. What technology resources, such as PowerPoint, Prezi, or graphic organizers, could be used for demonstrating "I Can" statements?

    c. How could you differentiate the requirements for different age groups/language groups?

5. Complete the "Resilience Checklist" below to discover how well your school is prepared to support and nurture students.

Resiliency Checklist

Creating an Environment That Fosters Resilience

How many of these key elements for fostering resilience are found in your school?

- ❑ The school is viewed as a safe and welcoming place for both ELs and their families.

- ❑ The school environment visually demonstrates that all cultures are welcome, through school décor and artifacts.

- ❑ Students and parents are made aware that the school is a caring environment, where ELs are respected and encouraged to openly share their language and culture.

- ❑ Students are viewed as assets to the school community, creating a mosaic of cultures represented.

- ❑ There is ongoing professional development for all personnel (both instructional and support state) to learn about cultural differences and learning/language challenges.

- ❑ There are clear and consistent schoolwide classroom academic expectations and behavioral boundaries.

- ❑ The school provides consistent and ongoing opportunities for all students to participate in meaningful classroom instructional and social interaction.

- ❑ The school teaches both academic and life skills.

- ❑ The school offers support and community connections for nonacademic problems.

- ❑ There is outreach into the community for members to serve as parent supports, translators, etc.

Source: Based on the work of Nan Henderson (2007, 2013)

5 PROVIDING SCHOOL–BASED SUPPORT FOR SIFE

CLASSROOM CHALLENGES

You're a seventh-grade science teacher in a crowded urban school in Los Angeles or Boston or Houston. In a noisy class of 35 adolescents, your students include a bright but shy Vietnamese girl who spent three years in a refugee camp; a bored, second-generation Chicano youth who often skips class; and a boy who has just arrived from rural El Salvador with a second-grade education.

How do you teach them all—and should you be required to? Do you isolate or "mainstream" the newcomers who have poor language skills? Do you group them by age or education level? Do you help them become literate in their native language, or skip straight to English? Should you treat them differently depending on their parents' legal status in this country?

All of these questions are being intensely debated across the country today as educators, community leaders and politicians grapple with the skyrocketing rate of immigrant children entering public schools, a widening popular backlash against the expense and special attention devoted to them, and continuing disagreements about the most effective way to help them succeed.

Does this sound like the introduction to an article about the current state of education? These are actually the opening three paragraphs of an article by Pamela Constable in *The Washington Post* on April 2, 1995. Other than which refugee groups are currently coming from the camps today, the issues and questions are essentially the same. More than 20 years later, the discussion of how best to meet the needs of these students continues.

SUPPORT SYSTEMS

This chapter is divided into two sections. We will look first at academic supports for new arrivals that focus on curriculum, pedagogy, and language development, and then also how schools can help these students with personal and social issues outside the classroom.

Academic Supports

Newcomer Programs

Consider these two quotations about the struggles many new arrivals face when they enter their new school:

> Cummins (2006) and Collier (1989) state that students with significant gaps in their formal schooling may need 10 years or more to acquire the academic language proficiency that will enable them to understand and express concepts and ideas that are relevant to long-term success in school—almost double the catch-up period predicted for students who have literacy skills in their first language. (*English Literacy Development*, 2014)

> Even though most immigrant students with limited schooling have a lot of catching up to do, they can achieve at break-neck speed if the work begins at a level they can understand. (Mace-Matluck, Alexander-Kasparik, & Queen, 1998, p. 24)

What can schools do to help these new arrivals catch up to the peers at this break-neck speed? One suggested remedy is to offer a **newcomer program**. A newcomer program is a specifically designed course or schedule with personnel, material, curriculum, and services selected to serve as a bridge between the skills and knowledge the students bring to their new school and the academic expectations of their peers. These programs may be one class, one strand of courses, or an entire school. The size and scope of the program will vary depending on the number of students, the resources of the district, and the academic gap of the students. Students with the least home language proficiency and the least previous education will require the most intense intervention.

A large-scale study of newcomer programs was conducted by the Center for Applied Linguistics in the 1990s (Short and Boyson, 2004 and 2012), and a follow-up study 10 years later listed some of the major components found in most newcomer programs:

- Acculturation to Western school system
- Develop or strengthen first-language literacy when possible
- Focus on literacy and language development in English
- Sheltered instruction in the major content subjects of math, science, and social studies
- Extended learning opportunities (after school, summer school, Saturday Enrichment)
- Connection to nonacademic services for the child and the family

Note: Details on the findings of these studies can be found on the Center for Applied Linguistics website and are available for free download at cal.org

Curriculum and Material for SIFE

Questions often arise from teachers and district administrators on the type of curriculum and material to use with **newcomers.** As with all educational decisions, the best answer is that the needs of the students must be foremost in the consideration. Some districts believe that all students must follow the state guidelines and standards for students based on their age, regardless of their English proficiency and prior schooling. However, for students with interrupted education, and especially those with little literacy in either their home or new language, this is extremely unrealistic. Of course, the state standards are the goal and the drive is to help the student reach that level as soon as possible. But students cannot be expected to stand on the floor and jump to the highest rung on the ladder without providing them the ability to reach each rung in between.

Although new arrivals and students with interrupted formal education (SIFE) are not special education students (except in specific circumstances), the idea of thinking in terms of modifications and accommodations is appropriate here. In a publication created by the *Ontario (Canada) Ministry of Education* (2014), the following distinction is recommended:

The Ministry recommends two types of support, depending on the skill level of the student and the gap in academic content knowledge: *modifications* for the students who have the least amount of English and previous schooling when the student is unable to "meet curriculum expectations" and *accommodations* when minor adjustments to expectations such as visual cues and extended time will be sufficient. (pp. 2–3)

Each school should consider every student individually, and decide whether modifications are appropriate and of what type, and if the student has sufficient content and language ability to access the curriculum with accommodations only. Some students may need modifications in some subjects but only accommodations in other classes, or they may move away from the need for modifications as the year progresses (*English Literacy Development*, 2014).

Literacy Development for SIFE

For students with interrupted schooling, and especially those with limited first-language literacy, a focus on developing reading skills is critical. The traditional maxim that students before Grade 3 are "learning to read" and that after Grade 3 they "read to learn" applies to native English speakers, but the general principle applies with new arrivals as well without the grade-level restrictions. Before these students can be expected to use their own literacy to understand academic subjects, they must first learn to extract meaning from text. For students with limited literacy, this means they must first learn to comprehend what they read.

The issue is that for upper elementary and secondary students, they do not have the luxury of taking 2 to 3 years to "learn to read" before they are expected to absorb new knowledge from classroom texts and lectures. One way to help students learn academic content while developing their reading skills is through the use of picture books.

Using Picture Books to Build Literacy and Content Knowledge

In the past, picture books were used by PreK–2 teachers to introduce story elements, book parts, and new vocabulary. Recently, however, there has been a proliferation of picture books produced with a focus on aspects of an academic topic, such as key American and world history events, mathematics concepts, and science principles, as well as sociocultural topics, focused on English learner school adjustment. Several published articles, blogs, and texts have indicated that picture books provide opportunities for teachers to build necessary concept and topic background for English learners Picture books introduce higher-order thinking skills, explain difficult academic concepts and vocabulary, both visually and verbally, as well as engage and instruct students with limited literacy, including newcomers with interrupted formal education.

Example Articles and Books Connecting Picture Books

- "A New Age for Picture Books" (*NJEA* Review)
- "Teachers Find Many Reasons to Use Picture Books with Middle and High School Students" (*School Library Journal*)
- *The Power of Picture Books: Using Content Area Literature in Middle School* (NCTE, 2009)
- *The Picture Book Experience: Choosing and Using Picture Books in the Classroom* (Pembroke Publishers Lit., 2009)

Criteria for Choosing Appropriate Picture Books for Content Instruction

Picture books for SIFE students need to be carefully chosen in order to provide substantial support for building background, introducing content concepts, **academic vocabulary**, and providing opportunities, through visuals and text, for academic oral language practice, and models of academic writing. There are some clear criteria for choosing picture books for English language arts, including story schema, characterization, inference through visuals and text, and providing rich plot lines to increase oral interaction and provide models for experiential writing.

For newcomers and SIFE learners, it is important for students to see themselves in the plot line of both fiction and nonfiction picture books.

Table 5.1   Choosing Picture Books/Multicultural Literature for English Language Arts

EL as Main Character	Meets Approaches Does Not Meet	Comments
Represents language learning as an active process; ELs are active learners, interacting with other students and/or the teacher.		
Language learning is a complex process; learning a new language takes time and effort by the student and facilitated by the teacher; some reference to SLA timeline.		
Newcomers bring their own funds of knowledge to the language learning process; narrative supports through examples students' own background knowledge, abilities, and experiences they bring to new learning.		

(Continued)

Table 5.1 (Continued)

EL as Main Character	Meets Approaches Does Not Meet	Comments
ELs do not abandon primary language and culture; learning supports both languages and cultures; no indication/inference that English is a superior language or that U.S. culture replaces native culture.		
Stages of adjustment; realistic portrait of students moving from culture shock to acculturation. Some stages and/or styles of adaptation represented in text.		
Illustrations represent an accurate, up-to-date view, unless reflecting a previous time period. Illustrations are not oversimplified generalizations of language or cultural group and do not visually represent stereotypes of the culture (e.g., male/female roles, housing, clothing, etc.).		
Additional information presented in the narrative, such as reasons for coming to the United States; self-concept and its impact on learning; fears of losing first language; roles and responsibilities in the family/culture, including, for example, adult–child roles and role reversals.		

Choosing picture books to introduce content topics, including mathematics, social studies, science, and technology requires a somewhat different set of criteria, including information that enhances background knowledge and introduces content topics, both visually and in print. This list will help you select the best books for introducing academic content to SIFE.

Table 5.2 Choosing Picture Books for Content Instruction

Questions to Consider Criteria for Each Question	Observations Evaluation
Does the picture book avoid race, gender, and/or ethnic stereotypes/stereotyping, including bias toward one point of view in presentation of historical information? • Accurate and balanced historical accounts through visual representations in photos, event descriptions, cultural images, historical figures, and artifacts. • Historical figure illustrations do not contain caricatures or narrative does not contain inaccurate representations of what historical figures accomplished.	

Questions to Consider Criteria for Each Question	Observations Evaluation
How is the information developed through text and illustrations? • *Illustrations and text information* on same page or companion pages. • *Content vocabulary* represented in text and/or visuals. • *Sentences*—a balanced variety from simple and compound. (Note: Most picture books rarely present complex and/or compound-complex sentences.) • Sentences contain *embedded phrasing* to explain or exemplify content vocabulary and/or concepts.	
Is the information accurately represented in text and visuals? Do text and visuals support age/grade appropriate learning of content information in mathematics and science? • Picture book text and visuals build background for and supports grade-level curriculum topics. • Picture book text and visuals expand on an aspect of the content to help newcomers develop an enriched understanding of the concepts to be learned (e.g., "Follow the drinking gourd" or other signals used to help slaves provides an enriched understanding of the Underground Railroad.)	
Does the content presented meet Common Core State Literacy or Mathematics Standards, National Social Studies Standards, or Next Generation Science Standards (NGSS)? • Correlations for Mathematics, Social Studies, and Science standards can be made between picture book content/theme/vocabulary and standard. • Science topic/themed picture books can be used with the NGSS 5-E Lesson Plan Model.	

Using Read-Alouds and Readers' Theater With SIFE Learners

- **Read Aloud/Think Aloud**

  Reading aloud has long been considered to be important for literacy development and reading success (Neuman, Copple, & Bredekamp, 2000). Students develop an understanding of the connection between the written word and its meaning. They learn, through teacher modeling, how to cluster phrases and clauses, focus on pausing, use **intonation,** as well as develop comprehension of text and vocabulary. Modeling and guiding the reading of small passages by teachers helps students understand and practice. In addition, read-alouds should be combined with think-alouds, also modeled by teachers, to enhance comprehension. Think-alouds help students become actively involved with text. Teachers model four types of text-comprehension think-alouds: connecting to self and one's own experiences; connecting to other stories, topics, texts, looking for connections between themes, character experiences, and/or events; connecting to the world, current and/or historic events (Harvey & Goudvis, 2009; Keene & Zimmerman; Tovani, 2000).

Sentence Stems for Text Connections Think Alouds:

Connecting to oneself: "This makes me think of a time I . . ."

Connecting to other stories (fiction): "We read another story about this"(plot, character, place, or time)

Connecting to content topic: "We studied this when we read . . ." (e.g., science, social studies, mathematics)

Connection to world events or experiences: "This makes me think of what I heard on TV, read about, or heard my parents talking about . . ."

- **Readers' Theater**
  Readers' Theater is a way to enhance text comprehension through dramatic oral presentation. In assigned roles students present a dialogue, taking turns and interacting with others. Students perform using their voices to depict characters from text, for example, based on the dialogue in a story. Students, other than characters from the story, can be assigned the role of narrators and dramatically read the narrative parts of the text for the presentation.

Readers' Theater provides students with the opportunity to develop fluency, appropriate intonation, expression, and inflection as well as enhance their comprehension through practice and performance of texts. Readers' Theater provides students with exposure to and interaction with science, social studies, and mathematic concepts and content topics and vocabulary.

Teacher Resources for Reader's Theater: Sierra, J. (1996). *Multicultural and Readers' Theater.* Phoenix, AZ: Oryz. There are also many free scripts for Readers' Theater available for download on the internet.

- **Wordless Books and SIFE Learners**

  Wordless picture books tell the story only through the pictures and illustrations. Careful viewing, page by page, provides students with the sequenced elements of the plot line, detailed visual information about the setting, and elements of characterization. Facial expressions, body language, placement of characters, objects, as well as shades of color, provide students with the clues leading to understanding of the sequence of events, time of day, place, emotions, and actions and/or feelings expressed by the characters.

Wordless picture books can be used to teach story elements. The plot line includes exposition (background information, including the introduction of the characters, setting, and time), rising action (building up to and introducing the problem/conflict), climax (the height of the problem), falling action (when the characters work toward solving the problem), and resolution (the end result of solving the problem and bringing the story to an end). With wordless picture books, all of these elements are presented through illustrations.

Wordless picture books are usually works of fiction. However, through various illustrations, photographs, paintings, and other visuals, teachers can find examples of or develop their own wordless books to explain content concepts in mathematics (problem solving), social studies (regional geography, historical events, constitutional law, etc.), and science (Newton's Laws of Motion, geology, how human organs function, planetary facts).

- **Sequencing and Building Oral Fluency**

  Students can learn to discuss the sequence of a story with picture books and begin to build oral language. First, introduce the vocabulary by pointing out and matching vocabulary with illustrations/pictures on each page. Modeling the language to express first, second, next, then and finally, the teacher can demonstrate how to retell events. Then students can work in pairs, **triads**, or small cooperative groups to practice the story order from a wordless book, using both the new vocabulary and sequence words.

Students can practice sequencing of events using **story frame** organizers with or without captions. Working in pairs, students can use the organizer and recreate the information in simple sketches. Adding captions can be accomplished by providing students **sentence starters** or **sentence frames** and a word bank. Picture frames can be cut apart and students can practice placing stories in order for oral practice. Organizing picture frames and retelling can be used as a formative assessment of fluency, ability to sequence events, and accurate use of new vocabulary.

Sheltered Instruction in Content Subjects

For students with some educational background, especially those with at least a limited amount of English language proficiency, another beneficial program is to provide content area subjects to be taught through sheltered instruction. Sheltered instruction has been used across the country for at least 30 years with English language learners. The idea behind sheltered instruction is that teachers, trained in an academic field such as math or science, teach the subject for which they are certified or licensed. Specific training is available to help these teachers know which pedagogical methods work best with ELs, such as adjusted pace, filling in gaps in background knowledge, specific use of visuals and modeling, and a focus on vocabulary.

Jana Echevarria, MaryEllen Vogt, and Deborah Short (1999) conducted a research study almost 20 years ago that looked at the effectiveness of sheltered instruction with English learners. Their study became the basis for what is now known as the SIOP Model: an acronym for Sheltered Instruction Observation Protocol. The authors of that study state, "[T]he goal was to create a framework that shows teachers how to integrate language and content instruction and identifies key elements that should be included in every lesson delivered to students learning content through a new language." (Short & Echevarria, 2016, p. 19). This model is still widely used today to help students learn academic subjects in a manner that takes their language proficiency into account.

Teachers consciously assist students in increasing their language skills at the same time that they are learning the content of the class, whether it is physical science, American history, or geometry. For students with interrupted education, this type of class is especially important. Time is the critical factor for them, and learning academic content at the same time that their English proficiency is increasing is invaluable.

Teaching to State Content and ELD Standards

Listed below is an example of a science lesson that combines the rigorous new standards required of all students with the use of picture books to teach a lesson on water conservation. Standards covered in the lesson are the following:

- **Next Generation Science Standards (NGSS)—Earth and Human Activity (5-ESS2.-2):** Describe and graph the amounts and percentages of water and fresh water in various reservoirs to provide evidence about the distribution of water on Earth.
- **Common Core State Standards—ELA Literacy R1.5.7:** Draw on information from multiple print or digital sources, demonstrating the ability to locate an answer to a question quickly or to solve a problem efficiently.
- **Common Core State Standards—Math MP 2:** Reason abstractly and quantitatively.

Next Generation Science Standards (NGSS) and the "5E Lesson Plan"

The 5E Lesson Plan Model (http://ngss.nsta.org/designing-units-and-lessons.aspx) has been designed to assist teachers in the development of science lessons to meet NGSS Standards and Benchmarks and facilitate understanding of key concepts and scientific vocabulary, as well as provide hands-on activities to question and explore concept learning. Each lesson includes five phases:

- Phase I: Engage—Focused on a "warm-up" activity to capture student attention, activate prior knowledge, and create key questions.
- Phase II: Explore—Focused on observing, exploring, and recording data. Students are involved in a hands-on activity to design and plan experiments, develop hypotheses, organize findings/results, and interpret data.
- Phase III: Explain—Focused on introduction of models, laws, theories, and connected vocabulary to understand and use to explain the results of their hands-on activities/experiments.
- Phase IV: Elaborate—Focused on opportunities for students to apply their acquired knowledge from the Explore and Explain Phases to new questions, new hypotheses, including related problems.
- Phase V: Evaluate—Focused on formative assessment, whether developed by teachers or based on student self-evaluation and used to check for understanding throughout the lesson and at the end of the lesson (e.g., ticket to leave, checklist, thumbs up/thumbs down, drawings, running records, etc.)

Sample 5E Science Lesson Using Picture Books: Water Conservation

LESSON STANDARDS	
Engage	Draw and illustrate a plot line for how drinking water reaches your home. Write 1–2 sentences describing the process. Use the picture on page 30 to help you write your own sentences. Did you know that all the water on the earth is the same water that's been here since the dinosaurs? What does that sentence tell you about water and the water that you use every day?
Explore	Teacher states: "Let's find out all about water for our state." Students will research and place data into their group's table or chart. Question prompts for group research at www.usgs.gov: What is the total water (ground water and surface water) in our state? What is the total estimated use of water? With your assigned group, take your specific activity from the "Activity Center": (1) As mayor, how would you save water? (2) How much water do you use at home? (3) How much water does a dripping faucet waste? (4) How much water does it take to grow a hamburger? (Water Content of Things) (5) How much is your daily indoor use? Additionally, picture books and book readings (see Appendix) provide background information for where do we find fresh water, water in our foods and water use in the home.
Explain	What does your data tell us about water use? Groups report out. Support for presentations provided by the teacher include picture book tables, illustrations, charts, and graphic organizers, sentence frames or sentence starters for oral response. Teacher states: "Now that we have heard all the reports, what do we want to learn about water and water conservation?" Teacher discusses the question and develops the hypothesis: What are some of the ways we use too much water every day? What are some of the ways we can conserve water?
Elaborate	Teacher provides students with a Water Use Diary. Students record water use in the home for one week using tools such as cups, jugs, buckets, etc. They return to class and review their water use. Students are prompted to examine their charts for how to reduce water consumption in their homes. Students, with teacher assistance, create a list of way to conserve. Using their charts to record changes made to save water.
Evaluate	Students present the changes they've made to save water in pairs or small groups. Teacher provides sentence stems or frames. Teacher keeps running records of student language use, including use of academic vocabulary when giving their oral reports. Additional assessments can include a "ticket out" oral response question, such as, name one way you have found to conserve water.

Source: Kaye, C. B., & Cousteau, P. (2013). *Make A Splash*!

Use of the observation checklist below can help teachers accurately assess how much the students are internalizing the content information and are able to express the new concepts in English. Since grading new arrivals is always a challenge, this type of assessment can be less threatening and more beneficial than the typical classroom test.

Table 5.3 Academic Performance Observation Checklist

Key: A = Always; O = Often; S = Sometimes; N = Never				
Criteria **Performance Expectations**	**A**	**O**	**S**	**N**
Can retell events accurately, in sequential order, using L1 or L2 (in one's own words, with manipulatives or through sequenced drawings).				
Seeking information: A. Can ask questions about concepts, vocabulary, sequenced information, etc. B. Can access resources to independently and/or with a peer to find answers to questions.				
Observant of text features (e.g., phrases, statements, and/or questions; use of vocabulary, embedded in phrasing, collocations, etc.) and replicate orally in responses and/or in writing, alone or with a peer.				
Observant of illustrations; can inference meaning from illustrations, through color, body language, facial expressions, layout, proxemics, etc. Can express understanding orally and/or in writing alone or with a peer.				
Can use content vocabulary orally and/or in writing sentences, with sentence stems, frames, or model through drawings, TPR, etc.				
Can make text-to-self connections from picture books about personal experiences.				
Can make text-to-text connections between picture books and other text readings, Internet sites, videos, visuals, class discussions, etc.				
Can make text-to-world connections between picture books and world knowledge from home country/culture or experienced in United States.				
Comments/Notes				

Following is a sample lesson outline that can be used for any subject. As encouraged by the SIOP Model (Echaviarria, Vogt, & Short, 2017), it begins with combining the state content standards with the state ELD standards. Each lesson should include vocabulary, essential background knowledge, and some type of activity to encourage use of the language to manipulate the content.

The building background portion of the lesson is especially critical for SIFE, because these students often are missing critical pieces of content knowledge. Even a short introduction to the topic through visuals, video clips, photos, or manipulatives can be invaluable.

Newcomer Lesson Outline

Lesson Preparation and Planning:

(*Utilize similar standards when possible and focus on those most critical.*)

State Content Standard/s:

State ELD Standard/s: (*Choose the ESL standard to be addressed and then determine the language needed to meet that standard. This becomes your specific lesson language objective.*)

Lesson Introduction: (*Find out what students already know, then fill in gaps with background knowledge necessary for lesson. Introduce a few key vocabulary terms and use them in context throughout the lesson.*)

Determine a short pre-assessment.

Key vocabulary (*Please limit new vocabulary to five words.*)

1.   2.   3.   4.   5.

Background knowledge required for lesson success and how best to introduce it:

Lesson Delivery: (*Include how to make the lesson interactive, specific questions that could be asked, grouping to be used, and activities that utilize all four domains.*)

Specific interactive activities

Questions to build thinking skills and determine understanding

Groupings to be used: whole class, small group, pairing, individual work, homework

Incorporation of all four domains

Lesson Wrap-Up: (*Formal or informal assessments to determine level of comprehension, consider how to re-teach what students did not understand.*)

Questions That Promote Language Development and Extended Response

Throughout the lesson, carefully crafted questioning strategies are important to help evaluate where the learner is in his or her comprehension of the lesson. Creating questions that require more than a yes/no answer encourage the newcomer to both demonstrate his or her understanding, as well as encourage him or her to ask questions to further his understanding of text. Salinas (2016, p. 48) described what she called **toxic questions**, which she indicates encourage learner passivity. The three key toxic questions she described were the following:

- Who can tell me something about today's lesson?
- Are there any questions?
- Does everyone understand?

Salinas (p. 48) proposed a series of "healthy" alternatives to the often overused toxic questions. These are questions that require more than a single word response, a nod, raised shoulders, and blank stares. Instead of the usual dead-end yes or no answer, these questions require tapping into metacognitive and cognitive connections to learning. For example, in place of a generic "what can you tell me," English learners are asked about their own thinking about the lesson and topic, with questions that tap not only into their knowledge, but also into the strategies used to come up with the answer:

1. What comes to your mind when you think of _____?

2. What made you think of that?

3. What strategies did you use to arrive at that answer?

Additionally students are asked about the "kinds" of questions they have, not only if they have any questions. Usually if asked, "Do you have any questions?" the answer is almost always no. English learners don't often feel comfortable asking questions. For newcomers, Salinas's model would need modification and a sentence starter or frame, which might look like "I have a question about _____ (how, why, when, or who) _____ this happened," for example.

Finally, teachers often ask, "Do you understand?" and "Do you have any questions?" English learners respond with a single-word response. In this case, English learners will respond yes, meaning they do understand when, in fact, they don't. Sometimes, English learners are uncomfortable asking a question and other times, they are not sure of what and how to ask about what they don't understand. A better request or series of requests requiring a response in various modalities (e.g., verbally, visually through drawing, physically through TPR actions, manipulating objects, writing using sentence stems/frames, word banks, etc.) to show what an English learner understands would include phasing in response to a "show me/tell me/describe for me what you understand."

Other Academic Supports Recommended for SIFE

Providing Heritage Language or Bilingual Language Support: The value of supporting and developing the native language literacy of second-language students has been clearly documented by both Cummins in his studies of Canadian language learners and by the three-decade long work of the husband and wife team of Wayne Thomas and Virginia Collier. Whenever possible, based on district resources and public policy, heritage language classes and/or bilingual classes are invaluable. They not only validate the cultures and languages of the students, but also provide a critical foundation for literacy development. Since almost three-fourths of all English learners in the United States are native Spanish speakers, providing courses in Spanish literacy is the logical solution for the majority of SIFE. For secondary-level students, this may be accomplished through heritage language classes. These courses are different than the typical Spanish I or II because they devote the majority of class time to reading and writing and literature, much the same way that English class for adolescents does not involve how to speak English. They are created specifically for students already comfortable with the basic vocabulary and conversation of Spanish. (For schools that do not have a sufficient number of native speakers for this type of course, placing the students in a level two or three class as a cluster could be a second-best alternative. However, simply putting a native speaker in a typical Spanish class may actually be detrimental, cause frustration, and possibly even lead to discipline problems.)

Assistance Meeting Graduation Requirements: Schooling in the United States and Canada is often vastly different from that of other countries. Even when a new arrival has attended several years of school in their home country, knowing what is expected for graduation here can be confusing. Most schools base completion on a combination of factors depending on state or provincial standards. Usually there is a list of required courses, some electives, and possibly a state-mandated exit exam or some other requirement such as volunteer hours, internships, or college entrance exam. Most middle and high schools have counselors or other personnel to help students make course selections, consider technical and career training options, prepare for high school exit or college entrance exams, and review career options. Many of the career opportunities available for new arrivals are unfamiliar and what will be required to enter these fields must be explained in detail. Unfortunately, in a typical secondary school each counselor may have a student load of up to 300 students. They often do not have the time, even when they understand the confusion for the new arrivals, to walk students through all the options available to them. In many instances, this responsibility falls to the ESL expert in the building.

> **Suggestion:** Find one counselor or graduation coach (or whoever in your building helps students make these decisions) and request that all SIFE students be assigned to this person. Because working with a student who is unfamiliar with the typical graduation process is more time consuming, this person should have a slightly smaller caseload.

Expanded Learning Opportunities Time is the most critical factor for students with limited or interrupted schooling, and one of the best ways to help make up for lost time is through programming that occurs outside typical school hours: Saturday, after school, or in the summer.

Listed below are three exemplary programs that offer students opportunities for language and literacy development.

Saturday Newcomer Academy in Oregon

The Saturday Newcomer Academy, an extended learning program for Newcomers Grades 5–12 in Beaverton, a suburb of Portland, Oregon, is aimed at accelerating language learning for new English learners and providing leadership opportunities for high school level former and advanced ELs. The academy was created for English learners who arrive in U.S. schools after fourth grade, because these students face the challenge of learning the language quickly while building the literacy and content knowledge they need for academic success.

Some of these "newcomers" come from interruptions in schooling (SIFE) or no school at all and must start from scratch, while others have skills and knowledge to transfer (Short & Boyson, 2012). They all need extra support to prosper in school and beyond. In this program, high school mentors and other volunteers work with the new arrivals on language development, with a focus on one-to-one oral language practice.

The curriculum is designed and coordinated by the ESL teachers, but the focus is on the peer interaction (Page, B., Personal Communication, June 14, 2016).

Global Village Project (GA) Summer Reading Program

The Global Village Project is a middle school near Atlanta designed to equip recently arrived refugee girls with the academic and social knowledge needed for success in a high school or equivalency program. The innovative approach to English language and literacy includes small classes, one-on-one literacy workshops, flexible guided reading groups, and thematic projects across content areas. The program also integrates STEAM—science, technology, engineering, arts, and mathematics—in its content teaching, focusing on expanding real-world learning for students. In addition to the integration of the arts throughout the content areas, students take classes in music, visual arts, drama, and dance.

One of the creators of the reading program, Mary Lou McCloskey, describes their summer reading club:

Refugee students are not likely to attend stimulating camps or go on exotic vacations in the summertime. Rather, they are at serious risk of summer regression in both their reading and oral English language proficiency. They often come from homes where they have access to few books, few models for reading, and little opportunity to hear and use English over the summer. The Global Village Project believes that summer reading, and talking about reading, can make an important difference. For three years now, the GVP Summer Book Club has been held in the Clarkston Community Library, close to the homes of most students. For seven years, this summer program has supported the girls as they listened to read-alouds from local celebrities; hear book talks from teachers and alumnae, read together, participated in reading activities with volunteers in small, leveled groups; and learned about and used the library to find and read books students love. Volunteers, with a school liaison, manage the program, transport students, lead groups and activities, bring snacks, and help in many other ways. The library provides support through both use of its venue and by helping to locate books and book sets from across the system for various groups; the school supports through providing books, resources, and a student intern. High-school level alumnae help out with set-up and leadership, and they are now managing their own group—choosing their own books and taking turns leading their group. (McCloskey, Personal Communication, June 27, 2016)

F.A.C.E. Time Family Reading Program in Lexington KY

F.A.C.E. Time is a combination of an after-school and summer reading program for elementary and middle school students and their families. The after-school program is dedicated to the development of academic skills as well as social/behavioral adaptation and cultural expression for children up to Grade 8. The F.A.C.E. Time Summer Program provides instruction in writing, music, mathematics, social studies, art, physical education, and cultural expression, as well as organized educational field trips. The social studies instruction focuses specifically on each of the countries represented by the children within the group.

The after-school program is augmented by the Prime Time Family Reading Program, which occurs in June and July. Each week, the families come together in the school library. The books are first read by a story-teller, and then discussed with the help of a scholar as facilitator with translators available. Adults as well as children participated actively in the discussions and were eager to receive and read the books. The school reports that the program has resulted in both increased literacy skills for the children and increased parental involvement in the education of their children (Cairo, Sumney, Blackman, & Joyner, 2012).

Nonacademic Supports

Connections to Social Services: One of the most important services that a school can provide is connecting new arrivals with people and organizations that can help them adjust to their new home and meet basic health and economic needs. Families that come as refugees have resettlement organizations that support the adults and children, at least during the first critical months. But many families and students who are undocumented have little or no support networks. Churches and some civic agencies provide assistance, but many of the typical social services that require government financial support are closed to these families. It is critical that schools find available organizations and make connections. Some schools have social workers to help make these links, while others use the counselor or other school personnel. In some communities, schools have informal quarterly meetings with social service organizations to make valuable connections. (Refugee resettlement groups are required by the federal government to meet quarterly with affected community agencies, including schools, where their clients are being settled.)

Many school districts have bilingual staff whose primary job it is to help parents understand the requirements of the new school system. However, their job often goes beyond simple translating and interpreting.

For many paraprofessionals, an additional and often unwritten part of their responsibilities includes assisting families with essentials such as finding food pantries, collecting winter clothing, connecting to legal services, and getting psychological and physical health care when needed.

Preparation for Postsecondary Options: As mentioned earlier in this chapter, preparing for graduation and then life after high school requires knowledge and assistance. Thinking about a potential career and then knowing how to obtain the skills and degrees to make that dream a reality takes years of planning. Some of that preparation occurs in the classrooms and counselors' offices, but much of it traditionally occurs in the home. For students whose parents are not familiar with the rigors of preparing for the postsecondary world, and especially for parents with limited educational backgrounds themselves, the intervention and assistance of a third-party may be helpful.

Many school districts have internal programs or allow external organizations to provide that support. Knowledge of financial support for students from specific ethnic backgrounds may make a critical difference in opening the door to college. Nonprofit groups may provide "college nights" that explain the college entrance process and help complete the FAFSA (Free Application for Federal Student Aid: fafsa.ed.gov) for those who qualify. They may assist with completing college applications and may even offer funding to help with the application fee.

> An essential factor in access to postsecondary education is obtaining "college knowledge"—that is, gaining an understanding of the complex processes of college admissions and finance in the United States—from undertaking appropriate college-preparatory work in high school and taking the SAT or ACT exams, to selecting and applying to suitable colleges, to locating and applying for various types of financial aid. . . . Immigrant high school students, many of whom are low-income and/or have parents who did not attend college, face the additional barriers of language difficulties and a general lack of familiarity with the American higher education system. (Erisman, & Looney, 2007)

Wrap-Around Services Needed, Helping the Whole Family

For many SIFE, difficulties and problems outside of school heavily impact their ability to attend school and to be able to concentrate on academics when present. Schools can help connect students to support systems outside of the school walls and at times are able to actually bring some of these critical services into the building. Listed below are two ways that some schools are offering assistance to students inside the school building and often during the regular school day.

In-School Free Store

A middle and high school for new arrivals in Columbus, Ohio, has set up a store on site for students to be able to shop for and "purchase" needed products such as school supplies, clothing, personal care items, and even food. The Student Success Store is being operated by a nonprofit organization and is underwritten by a grant from United Way. Students work in the store to gain experience in retail, and all products are available at no cost. Collaboration with community organizations, including the county food pantry, as well as support from local businesses ensures that the shelves remain well stocked.

School-Based Health Centers

One program that is being replicated across the United States to provide nonacademic support to students is the creation of health clinics inside the school building. These clinics, known as school-based health centers, often provide more services that the typical school nurse has been able to supply. According to the website of the Department of Health and Human Services ("Served Populations," 2016), "students and their families rely on school-based health centers to meet their needs for a full range of age-appropriate health care services, typically including primary health care, mental and behavior health care, dental and oral health, health education, substance abuse counseling, case management, and nutrition education." HHS estimates that up to 2,000 schools provide this type of service for students.

For Further Study

1. Look at what programming your school or school district currently offers for new arrivals. Research what other school districts around you are doing, as well as what is happening across the country. Check out these sources for information on Newcomer Programs: Center for Applied Linguistics (cal.org), International Network for Public Schools (internationalsnps.org), and the book *How to Design and Implement a Newcomer Program* (Custodio, 2011). How could you use some of these ideas to improve the programming you currently offer your students with interrupted education?

(Continued)

(Continued)

2. What social service agencies already have a connection to your school? Are there areas in which you need to reach out to community groups to find organizations that provide vital services your students and their families need? Does your school have regular contact with the organizations in your area to find out what new programs they offer? Create a list of community organizations in your area that provide services needed by your students.

3. Create a Readers' Theater lesson for your class. One option for this lesson is to use a picture book as the text for the activity, selecting one student to serve as narrator and assigning other students to read the dialogue of the characters in the story. Another option is to create an original script based on a topic covered in your class. Use the students to read from a script that incorporates key concepts and vocabulary from the lesson. You could arrange the class to appear to be a television studio, with students reading the "script" from a show about this lesson.

4. Consider developing a program that encourages your families to make more connections to the school. Some possible activities could include the following:
   • A family literacy night in which parents are provided with bilingual picture books that they can use to read to younger children
   • Creating bilingual reading kits that can be distributed to the students to encourage reading at home with the family
   • A program that prepares parents of preschoolers for the transition to kindergarten.
   • A program that helps high school students and their parents look at postsecondary options. It could include a visit to a local college, a FAFSA night, or a career night with businessmen who represent the cultures of the students.

GLOSSARY

Academic language: a learner's oral and written language, including vocabulary, sentence structure, grammar, punctuation, and discourse style, used in school interactions.

Academic vocabulary: the oral and written vocabulary used in classroom texts, discussions, and interactions related to academic content.

Coyote: a Spanish slang term used to describe a person who receives money for assisting immigrants attempting to cross the southern border from Mexico into the United States.

Culture shock: a feeling of disorientation as a result of a change in environment, experiencing a new way of life, or a set of beliefs different from one's own. English learners experiencing culture shock go through a series of phases before acculturation/adjustment to the new culture is achieved.

DACA: the acronym for Deferred Action for Childhood Arrivals. This "executive action" was issued by President Obama to aid children who came to the United States before their 16th birthday. These children are permitted to reside in the United States legally to work and/or attend post-secondary education. Details of the conditions for applying for DACA status can be found at http://www.immigrationequality.org/get-legal-help/our-legal-resources/path-to-status-in-the-u-s/daca-deferred-action-for-childhood-arrivals/.

Durable solution: the term used by the United Nations High Commission on Refugees to describe a long-term placement for a refugee, whether the refugee will eventually return to his or her home country, remain in the country of flight, or resettle in a third country.

ELD: an acronym for English Language Development. This term in used specifically for the development of English-language skills in conjunction with the development of academic skills in programs for English learners.

ELL: an acronym for English-language learner. It is a designation assigned to students for whom English is not their first language. Students may be placed in bilingual and/or English as a Second Language (ESL) programs to assist in the development of social and academic English skills. *Note:* Recently school districts across the United States have been using **EL**, or English learner, more frequently than ELL. The authors have chosen EL throughout the text as the preferred designation for English learners.

ESL: an acronym for English as a Second Language, programs designed for English learners to build both social and academic language skills. (In some U.S. states, the term ESOL, English to speakers of other languages, is used in place of ESL.)

Green card: is the government identity card used to indicate and identify that a person has permission to live and work in the United States.

Hispanic: describes a person who speaks Spanish as a native or first language, or whose heritage is based in a country or culture in which Spanish is the primary language.

I-94: the government document a refugee receives indicating he or she has been officially accepted into the United States. This document is used for approximately 1 year until a "green card" is received.

Immigrant: a person who leaves his or her native country to live in another country, usually with the intention of remaining and often applying for legal status and/or citizenship.

Intonation: a linguistics term identifying a variation of pitch or tone in speaking used for expression of attitude or emotion and used when asking a question, issuing a command, persuading, or expressing an opinion.

Latino: identifies a person who speaks a language based on the Latin language, specifically Spanish, French, and Portuguese in the Western hemisphere.

LEP: an acronym for limited English proficiency. This term was used for a number of years by educators and the U.S. Department of Education to describe students who were not yet proficient enough in English to be able to access classroom instruction without some level of support. The term has gone out of favor at all levels because of its emphasis on student limitations rather than student abilities.

Manipulatives: items such as buttons, markers, tiles, dice, plastic letters, sentence strips, picture sequences, students can move and utilize to assist when learning academic concepts and using academic language.

McKinney-Vento Homeless Education Improvement Act: the law that oversees the federal assistance of homeless people throughout the United States. McKinney-Vento provides support for homeless children with access to education and other services to ensure that homeless children have the same opportunities as other students to achieve academic standards. (See www2.ed.gov/policy/elsec/leg/esea02/pg116.html.)

Migration narrative: a story based on a person's move from one location to another. It is used as a strategy to help English learners validate their experiences, overcome culture shock, and acculturate to their new location.

Newcomer program: a set of classes or a curriculum designed to help new arrivals to the country orient to the present school and make the cultural and academic adjustment.

Newcomers: students who have just arrived from their birth country or another country, many with little or no apparent second-language skills, and frequently with limited native-language academic skills.

ORR: identifies the Office of Refugee Resettlement, a division of the Department of Health and Human Services. This division oversees the resettlement of refugees brought to the country through the State Department. (See www.acf.hhs.gov/orr.)

Picture books: books in which illustrations are an integral part of the narrative. Picture books are often shorter in length, with a specific fictional or factual theme or focus; the picture book genre may include themes and topics from literature, social studies, and science.

Plyler v. Doe: the Supreme Court case, decided in 1982, that prevents all P–12 schools from denying enrollment of children based on immigration status. (See www.uscourts.gov/educational-resources/educational-activities/access-education-rule-law.)

Political asylum: defines a refugee's request to be able to stay in a country outside one's native land, based on a claim of danger. (See www.uscis.gov/humanitarian/refugees-asylum/asylum/obtaining-asylum-united-states.)

Readers' Theater: an instructional use of dramatic reading, usually involving a text written in play format, in which students read aloud individual assigned passages with fluency and expression. Readers' Theater scripts have four to six roles and are read in a classroom setting without the inclusion of sets, props, or costumes.

Realia: artifacts that can be touched and handled by students to provide concrete examples of objects, such as foods, menus, clothing, and other objects used for a variety of tasks and occupations. Realia, or real objects, facilitate oral language production between students and between students and teacher.

Refoulement: from the French, is a term that refers to the danger a refugee may face upon returning to his or her home country if the situation that caused the departure has not been resolved.

Refugee: a person who, owing to well-founded fear of being persecuted for reasons of race, religion, nationality, membership of a particular social group or political opinion, is living outside the country of his or her nationality. The United Nations High Commission on Refugees determines the conditions that designate who is a refugee.

Repatriation: the act of returning, voluntarily, to one's home country, usually after being declared a refugee.

Resilience: the ability to recover from or adjust to change. For students who have experienced culture shock, trauma, tragedy, and/or significant stress, such as serious health problems or deaths of loved ones, as with immigrants, refugees, and/or students with interrupted formal education, it is the ability and the capacity to recover quickly from difficulties from past experiences. With the help of trained school personnel recovery can be accomplished.

Resiliency wheel: provides the key elements of resiliency building to address the needs of learners in a school setting. A resiliency wheel provides teachers with six key elements to help create a positive learning environment. The resiliency wheel is based on a body of resilience research. (See N. Henderson. in Havens of Resilience, at www.ascd.org/publications/educational-leadership/sept13/vol71/num01/Havens-of-Resilience.aspx.)

Section 504: a part of the Rehabilitation Act of 1973. It is a civil rights statute that prohibits discrimination, exclusion from participation in any school activity or program, based on a temporary or permanent disabling condition. These conditions substantially limit student participation when the student is measured against a non-disabled peer. This includes students with chronic illnesses, low vision, impaired hearing, movement disorders, conduct disorders, behavioral disorders, and/or disorders which temporarily disable a child. Both modifications and accommodations are determined to help students successfully participate in academic and social school activities. (See http://www.greatschools.org/gk/articles/section-504-2/ for a sample list of accommodations.)

Sentence frames: scaffolds that provide the basic structure of a sentence, with strategically placed blanks into which a student adds a key vocabulary word, a key concept, or use compare/contrast or persuasive language to complete a prompt. Sentence frames assist English learners in formulating a complete thought.

Sentence starters: similar to sentence frames. With sentence starters, only the beginning of the sentence is provided to help students express a key concept, supporting idea, or define a vocabulary term.

SIFE: an acronym for students with interrupted formal education. SIFE learners have experienced interruptions in first-language education in their home country due to a number of circumstances, such as war, terrorism, lack of financial resources, religious or racial persecution, or family circumstances. (**SLIFE**, a more recently used acronym for students with limited or interrupted formal education, adds a focus on students who also have limited literacy in their home language.)

Story frames: provide the basic outline of a story, with key introductory words or phrases so that students can use inference skills, prior knowledge, or learning to sequentially complete the frames to develop a narrative.

SWIS: an acronym for Settlement Workers in Schools, a Canadian government program that places case workers in the schools with large numbers of refugee children. The workers serve as liaisons between the school and the families of the children. (See www.tvdsb.ca/programs.cfm?subpage=123449.)

Toxic questions: questions that permit and may even encourage learner passivity. Toxic questions require no more than a single word response, a nod, raised shoulders, and discourage extended discourse needed to practice oral academic language. (See *Multilingual Educator* [2016], at www.gocabe.org/wp-content/uploads/2016/03/ME2016.pdf.)

TPR: an acronym for total physical response. It is a language-teaching method developed by James Asher (1969) that combines learning vocabulary with commands, movement, and activity.

TPS: an acronym for Temporary Protective Status. It is an immigration status granted to eligible nationals of countries with citizens designated as in need of this protection. Holders of this status are permitted to stay and to work for a certain period of time because conditions in the home country make it dangerous or inadvisable for nationals to return, including natural disasters, political uprisings, and so on. (See www.uscis.gov/humanitarian/temporary-protected-status.)

Trauma: a physical or emotional deeply disturbing experience, possibly leading to long-term cognitive, physical, and/or emotional difficulties.

Triads: in education, it refers to creating student groups consisting of three members. Students may be grouped homogeneously by first/native lingual, language development, academic ability, or heterogeneously.

Unaccompanied minors: the general term for the children who cross the border without the protection of a parent or guardian. The term usually refers to children who cross the southern border with Mexico, but it can also refer to other minors who enter the United States alone. (The term UAC or Unaccompanied Alien Child is the government term for such children.)

UNHCR: the United Nations High Commission on Refugees, the division of the United Nations that oversees the safety and possible resettlement of refugees. (See www.unhcr.org/en-us.)

VOLAG: an acronym for Volunteer Agency, which refers to the nine national agencies that resettle refugees in the United States. (See www.acf .hhs.gov/orr/resource/voluntary-agencies.)

WIDA: an acronym for World-Class Instructional Design and Assessment. It represents a consortium of 39 states whose departments of education have banded together to develop English proficiency standards and assessments that are used across the Consortium. (See www.wida.us.)

APPENDIX A

PICTURE BOOK RESOURCES FOR 5E SCIENCE LESSON ON WATER CONSERVATION

Butzow, J., & Butzow, C. (2000). *Science through children's literature: An integrated approach.* Portsmouth, NH: Teacher Ideas Press.

Ganeri, A. (2005). *Down the drain: Conserving water (you can save the planet).* Chicago, IL: Heinemann.

Green, J. (2005). *Why should I save water?* Hauppauge, NY: Barrons Educational Services.

Hooper, M., & Coady, C. (2015). *The drop in my drink: The story of water on our planet.* London, UK: Frances Lincoln Children's Books.

Kaye, C. B., & Cousteau, P. (2012). *Make a splash! A kid's guide to protecting our oceans, lakes, rivers, and wetlands.* Minneapolis, MN: Free Spirit Publishing.

Kerley, B. (2006). *A cool drink of water.* National Geographic Children's Books.

Locker, T. (1997). *Water dance.* New York, NY: Houghton Mifflin Harcourt.

McKinney, B. (1998). *A drop around the world.* Nevada City, CA: Dawn Publications.

Miyares, D. (2015). *Float.* New York, NY: Simon and Schuster Books for Young Readers.

Paul, M. (2015). *Water is water: A book about the water cycle.* New York, NY: Roaring Book Press.

Rajinsky, N. M., & John, M. (2003). *Water up, down, and all around.* North Mankato, MN: Capstone Publishers.

Strauss, R. (2007). *One well: The story of water on earth (CitizenKid).* Toronto, Canada: Kids Can Press.

Wick, W. (1997). *A drop of water.* New York, NY: Scholastic Press.

APPENDIX B
LIST OF RECOMMENDED PICTURE BOOKS FOR USE WITH SIFE

Adjustment to School/Learning English/Value of Education

Anzaldua, G. (1997). *Friends from the other side/Amigos del otro lado*. San Francisco, CA: Children's Book Press. (In English and Spanish.)

Aliki. (1998). *Mariantha's story: Painted words and spoken memories*. New York, NY: Greenwillow Books.

Bunting, E. (2001). *Dreaming of America: An Ellis Island story*. Mahwah, NJ: Troll Communications.

Bunting, E. (2006). *One green apple*. New York, NY: Clarion Books.

Choi, Y. (2003). *The name jar*. New York, NY: Dragonfly Books.

Elya, S. M. (2006). *Home at last*. New York, NY: Lee and Low Books.

Garland, S. (1997). *The lotus seed*. Boston, MA: HMH Books for Young Readers.

Hest, A. (2003). *When Jesse came across the sea*. Somerville, MA: Candlewick.

Hoffman, M. (2012). *The color of home*. London, UK: Francis Lincoln.

Jimenez, F. (2000). *La Mariposa*. New York, NY: Houghton Mifflin.

Jules, J. (2007). *No English*. Ann Arbor, MI: Mitten Press.

Levine, E. (1995). *I hate English*. New York, NY: Scholastic Paperbacks.

Mobine-Uddin., A. (2005). *My name is Bilal*. Honesdale, PA: Boyds-Mill Press.

Park, F. (2012). *Where on earth is my bagel?* New York, NY: Lee and Low Books.

Perez, A. I. (2013). *My diary from here to there. Mi diario de aqui hasta Alla*. San Francisco, CA: Children's Book Press. (In English and Spanish.)

Recoorvitis, H. (2014). *My name is Yoon*. New York, NY: Square Fish.

Rodriguez, L. J. (1998). *America is her name*. Evanston, IL: Curbstone Books.

Say, A., (2008). *Grandfather's journey*. Boston, MA: HMH Books for Young Readers.

Stanek, M. (1989). *I speak English for my mom*. Park Ridge, IL: Albert Whitman & Co.

Stojic, M. (2002) *Hello world: Greetings in 43 languages around the world*. New York, NY: Scholastic.

Wells, R. (1989). *Streets of gold*. New York, NY: Dial Publishers.

Wells, R. (2009). *Yoko*. Burbank, CA: Disney-Hyperion.

Williams, K. (2009). *My name is Sangoel*. Grand Rapids, MI: Eerdmans Books for Young Readers.

Williams, K. L. (2016). *Four feet, two sandals*. Grand Rapids, MI: Eerdmans.

Basic Concept Books (alphabet, numbers, colors and shapes, parts of the body, clothing, senses, seasons, weather, school, transportation, family, etc.)

Aliki. (1989). *My five senses*. New York: NY: Harper Trophy.

Carle, E. (1994). *The very hungry caterpillar*. New York, NY: Philomel Books.

Carle, E. (1996). *Brown bear, brown bear*. New York, NY: Henry Holt & Co.

Carle, E. (2007). *Slowly, slowly, said the sloth*. London, UK: Puffin Books.

Kovalski, M. (1987). *The wheels on the bus*. Boston, MA: Joy Street Books.

Kubler, A. (2002). *Head, shoulders, knees and toes*. Child's Play International.

Morris, A. (1989). *Bread, bread, bread*. New York, NY: Scholastic.

Morris, A. (2001). *Houses and homes*. New York, NY: Harper Collins.

Toms, K. (2009). *Old MacDonald had a farm*. Berkhamsted, UK: Make Believe Books.

Alphabet Books (available on practically every subject)

Ada, A. F., & Silva, S. (2001). *Gathering the sun*. New York, NY: Rayo. (In Spanish.)

Cooper, E. (2015). *An animal alphabet*. New York, NY: Orchard Books.

Ehlert, L. (1989). *Eating the alphabet: Fruits and vegetables from A to Z*. San Diego, CA: Harcourt Brace.

Herman, S. (2003). *Mexico ABCs*. Minneapolis, MN: Picture Window Books.

Krebs, L. (2004). *We all went on safari*. Cambridge, MA: Barefoot Books.

Onyefulu, I. (1997). *A is for Africa*. London, UK: Puffin Books.

Schwartz, D. (2000). *G is for Googol: A math alphabet book*. New York, NY: Tricycle Press.

Wildsmith, B. (2009). *Brian Wildsmith's amazing animal alphabet*. Cambridge, MA: Star Bright Books.

Counting Books

Arena, J., & Gilpin, S. (2013). *100 snowmen*. New York, NY: Lions Publishers.

Falwell, C. (1995). *Feast for 10*. Boston, MA: HMH Books for Young Readers.

Hutchins, P. (1989). *The doorbell rang*. New York, NY: Greenwillow Books.

McGrath, B. (1994). *The M & M's counting book*. New York, NY: Scholastic.

Milbourne, A. (2008). *How big is a million?* London, UK: Usborne Publishers Limited.

Ross, T. (2003). *Centipede's one hundred shoes*. New York, NY: Henry Holt & Co.

Shahan, S., & Barragan, P. (2005). *Cool cats counting*. Atlanta, GA: August House Publishers.

Stiegemeyer, J. (2008). *Gobble, gobble, crash: A barnyard counting bash*. New York: NY: Dutton Children's Books.

Mathematics concept books

Adler, D., & Miller, E. (2010). *Fractions, decimals, and percents*. New York, NY: Holiday House.

Adler, D., & Miller, E. (2013). *Perimeter, area, and volume: A monster book of dimensions*. New York, NY: Holiday House.

Adler, D., & Miller, E. (2000). *Shape up! Fun with triangles and other polygons*. New York, NY: Holiday House.

Calvert, P. (2011). *The multiplying menace divides*. Watertown, MA: Charlesbridge.

Calvert, P. (2006). *Multiplying menace: The revenge of Rumplestilskin*. Watertown, MA: Charlesbridge.

Demi. (1997). *One grain of rice*. New York, NY: Scholastic.

Dodds, D. A. (2005). *The great divide: A mathematical marathon*. Somerville, MA: Candlewick.

Shaskan, T. S. (2008). *If you were a fraction*. Minneapolis, MN: Picture Window Books.

Tang, G. (2004). *The grapes of math*. New York, NY: Scholastic Paperbacks.

Colors and Shapes Books

Bijsterbosch, A. (2015). *Chameleon sees colors*. New York, NY: Clavis.

Chernesky, F. S. (2013). *Pick a circle, gather squares: A fall harvest of shapes*. Park Ridge, IL: Albert Whitman & Co.

Khan, H. (2015). *Golden domes and silver lanterns: A Muslim book of colors*. San Francisco, CA: Chronicle Books.

Loughrey, A. (2010). *Circles (shapes around me)*. London, UK: QEB Publishing.

Loughrey, A. (2010). *Shapes around me: Squares*. London, UK: QEB Publishing.

Shahan, S. (2007). *Spicy, hot colors*. Atlanta, GA: August House.

Wordless Books (appropriate for teaching narration, building oral literacy; appropriate for older newcomers and parent–child storytelling in native language)

Banyai, I. (1998). *Zoom* (K–3). London, UK: Puffin Books.

Becker, A. (2013). *Journey* (ages 4–8). Somerville, MA: Candlewick.

Becker, A. (2014). *Quest* (ages 4–8). Somerville, MA: Candlewick.

Becker, A. (2016). *Return* (ages 4–8). Somerville, MA: Candlewick.

Boyd, L. (2014). *Flashlight* (ages 2–6). San Francisco, CA: New York, NY: Random House Books for Young Learners.

dePaola, T. (1978). *Pancakes for breakfast* (ages 4–7). Boston, MA: HMH Books for Young Readers.

Lehman, B. (2004). *The red book* (Pre-K–3/ages 4–7). Boston, MA: HMH Books for Young Readers.

Lehman, B. (2006). *Museum trip*. Boston, MA: HMH Books for Young Readers.

Miyares, D. (2015). *Float*. New York, NY: Simon & Schuster Books for Young Readers.

Pinkney, J. (2009). *The lion and the mouse*. New York, NY: Little Brown Books for Young Learners.

Schones, P. (2004). *Breakfast for Jack*. Honesdale, PA: Front Street.

Tan, S. (2007). *The arrival* (ages 12–adult). New York, NY: Arthur A. Levine Books.

Thomson, B. (2010). *Chalk* (ages 3–7). New York, NY: Two Lions.

Weisner, D. (1991). *Free fall*. New York, NY: Harper Collins

Weisner, D. (2006). *Flotsam*. Boston, MA: Clarion Books.

Weisner, D. (2011). *Tuesday*. Boston, MA: HMH Books for Young Readers.

Folk and Fairy Tales

Brett, J. (1999). *Gingerbread baby*. New York, NY: Scholastic.

Kimmel, E. (2000). *The runaway tortilla*. Cape Coral, FL: Winslow Press.

Ward, J. (2007). *There was a coyote who swallowed a fly*. Lanham, MD: Rising Moon Books.

Young, E. (1989). *Lon Po Po: A Little Red Riding Hood story from China*. New York, NY: Philomel Books.

Social Studies: Community, History, and Biography

Chesanow, N. (1995). *Where Do I Live?* Hauppauge, NY: Barrons.

Guthrie, W., & Jakobsen, K. (1998). *This land is your land*. New York, NY: Scholastic.

Knight, M. (2000). *Africa is not a country*. Minneapolis, MN: Millbrook Press.

Maestro, B. (1996). *Coming to America*. New York, NY: Scholastic.

Winter, J. (2005). *Librarian of Basra*. New York, NY: Simon and Schuster.

Winter, J. (2014). *Malala/Iqbal*. New York, NY: Simon and Schuster.

Science

Bang, M., & Chisholm, P. (2009). *Living sunlight: How plants bring the earth to life*. New York, NY: Blue Sky Press.

Carle, E. (2001). *The tiny seed*. New York, NY: Aladdin.

Cherry, L. (1990). *The great kapok tree*. San Diego, CA: Harcourt Brace.

Lawlor, L. (2012). *Rachel Carson and her book that changed the world*. New York, NY: Holiday House.

Language Arts

Bing, C. (2001). *The midnight ride of Paul Revere*. Brooklyn, NY: Handprint Books.

Cronin, D. (2003). *Diary of a worm*. New York, NY: Harper Collins.

Yamada, K. (2013). *What do you do with an idea?* Seattle, WA: Compendium.

Cultures of the Students

Cohn, D. (2009). *Namaste!* Great Barrington, MA: Steiner Books.

King, D. (2010). *I see the sun in Nepal.* Hardwick, MA: Satya House Publications.

Sockman, B. (2013). *Nepal adventure.* Lexington, KY: Building Peace Through Global Literacy.

REFERENCES

Abrego, L. J. (2014). I can't go to college because I don't have papers. In A. Darder and R. D. Torres (Eds.), *Latinos and education: A critical reader*. New York, NY: Routledge.

Advocates for Children of New York. (2010, May). Students with interrupted formal education: A challenge for New York City Public Schools.

Alber, R. (2016, June). 3 end-of-year reflection strategies for students. *Edutopia*. Retrieved February 17, 2017, from https://www.edutopia.org/blog/3-end-year-reflection-strategies-students-rebecca-alber

Alcala, A. (2000). The preliterate student: A framework for developing an effective instructional program. *ERIC Digest*.

American Community Survey. (2014). U.S. Bureau of the Census.

August, D., & Shanahan, T. (Eds.). (2006). *Developing literacy in second-language learners*. Washington, DC: Center for Applied Linguistics.

Bashir-Ali, K., & Custodio, B. (2002, April 11). Are we failing the ESL refugee student? Presentation at TESOL Convention. Salt Lake City, UT.

Bhutanese refugees in Nepal. (2007, October). Washington, DC: Cultural Orientation Resource Center at the Center for Applied Linguistics.

Birman, D. (2012, July 31). *Refugee children with low literacy skills or interrupted education: Identifying challenges and strategies*. Spring Institute for Intercultural Learning.

Brown, C. S. (2015). *The educational, psychological, and social impact of discrimination on the immigrant child*. Washington, DC: Migration Policy Institute.

Cairo, A., Sumney, D., Blackman, J., & Joyner, K. (2012, Winter). F.A.C.E. Time (Families and Communities Educating): Accommodating newcomers in elementary school. *Multicultural Education, 19*(2), 55–58.

Camarota, S. A. (2005, December). *Immigrants at mid-decade: A snapshot of America's foreign-born population in 2005*. Center for Immigration Studies.

Capps, R., Castañeda, R. M., Chandry, A., & Santos, R. (2007). *Paying the price: The impact of immigration raids on America's children*. Washington, DC: National Council of La Raza.

Castañeda, X., Felt, E., Martinez-Taboada, C., Castañeda, N., & Ramirez, T. (2013). Migratory stress and mental health in adolescent and young adult Mexican immigrants living in the United States: Contextualizing acculturation. In J. Ho (Ed.), *Immigrants: Acculturation, socioeconomic challenges and cultural psychology*. New York, NY: Nova Publishers.

Chang, H. N.-L. (1990). *Newcomer programs: Innovative efforts to meet the educational challenges of immigrant students*. San Francisco: California Tomorrow Immigrant Students Project.

Chaudry, Ajay, Capps, R., Pedroza, J. M., Castañeda, R. M., Santos, R., & Scott, M. M. Facing our future: Children in the aftermath of immigration enforcement. Washington, DC: Urban Institute. 2010. Retrieved from http://www.urban.org/publications/412020.html

Child Trauma Toolkit for Educators. (2008, October). National Child Traumatic Stress Network Schools Committee. National Center for Child Traumatic Stress. Los Angeles, CA and Durham, NC.

Children and education in refugee camps. (n.d.). Module 4 of Refugee Health Online Course. Retrieved from http://www.uniteforsight.org

Children of immigrant families. (2005, February 25). Center for Health and Health Care in Schools: Washington, DC.

Children of immigrants and refugees: What the research tells us. (2011, April). Fact sheet (Health and Health Care in Schools). George Washington University. Washington, DC.

Cloud, N., Genesee, F., & Hamayan, E. (2009). *Literacy instruction for English language learners: A teacher's guide to research-based practices*. Heinemann: Plymouth, NH.

Collier, V. (1989). How Long? A synthesis of research on academic achievement in a second language. *TESOL Quarterly, 23*, 509–531.

The Colombian diaspora in the United States. (2014, July). Migration Policy Institute.

Constable, P. (1995, April 2). Teaching America's newcomers: Immigrants in the classroom. *The Washington Post: Education Review*, pp. 1–8.

Convention relating to the status of refugees. (1951, July 28). Geneva, Switzerland: United Nations.

Costello, A., & Bebic, S. (2006, March). *Cultural orientation for refugees*. Center for Applied Linguistics, Washington, DC.

Cortina, R. (2009). Immigrant youth in high school: Understanding educational outcomes for students of Mexican origins. In T. Wiley, J. S. Lee, & R. Rumberger (Eds.), *The Education of Language Minority Immigrants in the United States*. Bristol, England: Multilingual Matters.

Crandall, J., Jaramillo, A., Olsen, L., & Kreeft Peyton, J. (2001). Diverse teaching strategies for immigrant children. In R. Cole (Ed.). *More strategies for educating everybody's children*. Alexandria, VA: ASCD.

Crosnoe, R., & Lopez Turley, R. N. (2011, Spring). K–12 educational outcomes of immigrant youth. *Future of Children Journal, 21*(1), 129–152.

Cummins, J. (1981). Age on arrival and immigrant second language learning in Canada: A reassessment. *Applied Linguistics, 11*(2), 132–149.

Cummins, J. (1981). The role of primary language development in promoting educational success for language minority students. In California State Department of Education (Ed.), *Schooling and language minority students: A theoretical framework* (pp. 3–49). Los Angeles, CA: National Dissemination and Assessment Center.

Custodio, B. (2011). *How to design and implement a newcomer program.* Boston, MA: Allyn and Bacon.

Davis, J. S. (Dec. 2013–Jan. 2014). Building resilient students: Three strategies for success. *Educational Horizons, 92,* 21–25.

DeCapua, A., & Marshall, H. (2010, March). Serving ELLs with limited or interrupted education: Intervention that works. *TESOL Journal, 1*(1), 49–70.

DeCapua, A., & Marshall, H. W. (2011). *Breaking new ground: Teaching students with limited or interrupted formal education in U.S. secondary schools.* Ann Arbor: University of Michigan Press.

DeCapua, A., Smathers, W., & Tang, L. F. (2009). Meeting the needs of students with limited or interrupted schooling. Ann Arbor: University of Michigan.

Deferred action for childhood arrivals: A guide for educators and support staff. (2014). Washington, DC: American Federation of Teachers.

DeNisco, A. (2015, September 18). Immigrant surge slows, but challenges remain for schools. *District Administration.*

Echevarria, J., Vogt, M., & Short, D. (1999). *Making content comprehensible for English learners: The SIOP model.* Boston, MA: Allyn and Bacon.

Echevarria, J., Vogt, M., & Short, D. (2017). *Making content comprehensible for English learners: The SIOP model* (5th ed.) Boston, MA: Allyn and Bacon.

English literacy development: Supporting English language learners with limited prior schooling. (2014, April). Ottawa, Ontario: Ontario Ministry of Education. Retrieved from http://edu.gov.on.ca/eng/literacynumeracy/inspire/research/CBS_LiteracyDevelop.pdf

Erisman, W., & Looney, S. (2007, April). *Opening the door to the American Dream: Increasing higher education access and success for immigrants.* Washington, DC: Institute for Higher Education Policy.

Faltis, C., & Coulter, C. (2008). Teaching English learners and immigrant students in secondary schools. Upper Saddle River, NJ: Pearson.

Fee, S. (2014, September 21). Promising Roma crackdown, far-right party gains ground in Hungary. Interview on NewsHour on pbs.org.

Fieser, E. (2015, June 30). After Dominican Republic pulls up welcome mat, Haitians ask "What next?" *Christian Science Monitor.*

Flaitz, J. (2006). *Understanding your refugee and immigrant students: An educational, cultural, and linguistic guide.* Ann Arbor: University of Michigan Press.

Focus on SLIFE: Students with Limited or Interrupted Formal Education. (2015, May). Madison, WI: WIDA Consortium.

Francis, D., Rivera, M., Lesaux, N., Kieffer, M., & Rivera, H. (2006). *Practical guidelines for the education of English language learners: Research-based recommendations for serving adolescent newcomers.* Portsmouth, NH: RMC Research Corporation, Center on Instruction. Retrieved from http://www.centeroninstruction.org/files/ELL2-Newcomers.pdf

Freeman, Y., & Freeman, D. (2002). *Closing the achievement gap: How to reach limited-formal-schooling and long-term English learners.* Portsmouth, NH: Heinemann.

Friedlander, M. (1991, Fall). The newcomer program: Helping immigrant students succeed in U.S. schools. *NCBE Program Information Guide Series,* 8.

Fry, R. (2005, November 1). *The higher drop-out rate of foreign-born teens: The role of schooling abroad.* Washington, DC: Pew Research Center.

Gándara, P. (2015). *The implications of deeper learning for adolescent immigrants and English language learners.* Students at the Center: Deeper Learning Research Series. Boston, MA: Jobs for the Future.

Garcia Coll, C., & Kerivan Marks, A. (Eds.). (2012). *The immigrant paradox in children and adolescents: Is becoming an American a developmental risk?* Washington, DC: American Psychological Association.

Gonzales, R. G. (2012). In spite of the odds: Undocumented immigrant youth, school networks, and college success. In C. G. Coll & A. Kerivan Marks (Eds.), *The immigrant paradox in children and adolescents: Is becoming an American a developmental risk?* Washington, DC: American Psychological Association.

Governments pledge to take in around 100,000 Syrian refugees. (2014, December 2). Geneva, Switzerland: United Nations High Commission on Refugees.

Grotberg, E. H. (1995). *A guide to promoting resilience in children: Strengthening the human spirit—Early childhood development: Practice and reflections number 8.* The Hague, the Netherlands: Bernard van Leer Foundation.

Grotberg, E. H. (1995). The international resilience project: research and applications. University of Alabama at Birmingham: Civitan International Research Center. [ED 423 955]

Hamayan, E. (1994). Language development of low-literacy students. In Fred Genesee (Ed.), *Educating second language children: The whole child, the whole curriculum, the whole community.* Cambridge, England: Cambridge University Press.

Harvey, S., & Goudvis, A. (2009). *Strategies that work: Teaching comprehension to enhance understanding* (2nd ed.). Portland, ME: Stenhouse.

Haynes, J. (2007). *Getting started with English language learners: How educators can meet the challenge.* Alexandria, VA: ASCD.

Health concerns in Ethiopia camps, start of school year for refugee children in Dadaab. (2011, September 2). Geneva, Switzerland: United Nations High Commission on Refugees.

Henderson, N. (2007). *Resiliency in action: Practical ideas for overcoming risks and building strengths in youth, families, and communities.* Solvang, CA: Resiliency in Action.

Henderson N. (September, 2013). Havens of resilience. *Educational Leadership,* 71(1), 22–27.

Henderson, N., & Milstein, M. M. (2003). *Resiliency in schools: Making it happen for students and educators.* Thousand Oaks, A: Corwin.

Hernandez, D. J. (2004). Demographic change and the life circumstances of immigrant families. *Future of Children, 14,* 17–47.

Hernandez, D. J., Denton, N. A., McCartney, S., & Blanchard, V. (2012). Children in immigrant families: Demography, policy, and evidence for the immigrant paradox. In Cynthia Garcia Coll and Amy Kerivan Marks (Eds.), *The immigrant paradox in children and adolescents: Is becoming an American a developmental risk?* Washington, DC: American Psychological Association.

Hill, N. E., & Torres, K. (2010). Negotiating the American dream: The paradox of aspirations and achievement among Latino students and engagement between their families and schools. *Journal of Social Issues, 66*, 95–112.

The Hispanic population: 2010 census briefs. (2011, May). U.S. Census Bureau: Washington, DC.

Ho, S. (2005). Caring for Syrian refugee children: A program guide supporting the care and settlement of young immigrant children. Retrieved from http://www.cmascanada.us

How to support refugee students in the ELL classroom. (2008). *Colorin Colorado.* Retrieved from http://www.colorincolorado.org/article/23379?theme=print

Immigrant students and secondary school reform: Compendium of best practices. (2004). Washington, DC: The Council of Chief State School Officers.

In historic shift, new migration flows from Mexico fall below those from China and India. (2015, May 21). Washington, DC: Migration Policy Institute.

In-country refugee/parole program for minors in El Salvador, Guatemala, and Honduras with parents lawfully present in the United States. (2014, November 14). Fact Sheet from U.S. Department of State and U.S. Department of Homeland Security.

Irizarry, J. G., & Antrop-González, R. Ricanstructing the discourse and promoting school success: Extending a theory of culturally responsive pedagogy for diasporicans. In Antonia Darder and Rodolfo D. Torres (Eds.), *Latinos and Education: A Critical Reader.* New York, NY: Routledge.

Jimenez, F. (1997). *The circuit: Stories from the life of a migrant child.* Albuquerque, NM: University of New Mexico Press.

Jimenez, F. (2002). *Breaking through.* Boston, MA: HMH Books for Young Readers.

Jimenez, F. (2009). *Reaching out.* Boston, MA: HMH Books for Young Readers.

Jimenez, F. (2015). *Taking hold.* Boston, MA: HMH Books for Young Readers.

Kapteijns, L., & Arman, A. (2008). Educating immigrant youth in the United States: An exploration of the Somali case. *Bildhaan: An International Journal of Somali Studies, 4*(6).

Kaye, C. B., & Cousteau, P. (2013). *Make a splash!* Minneapolis, MN: Free Spirit Publishing.

Keene, E. O. & Zimmerman, S. (1997) *Mosaic of thought: Teaching comprehension in a reader's workshop.* Portsmouth, NH: Heinemann.

Kremer, J. D., Moccio, K. A., & Hammell, J. W. (2009). *Severing a lifeline: The neglect of citizen children in America's immigration policy.* Washington, DC: Urban Institute.

Krogstad, J. M. (2015, July 1). Puerto Rico's losses are not just economic, but it people, too. Washington, DC: Pew Research Center.

Krogstad, J. M., & Passel, J. S. (2014, November 18). *Five facts about illegal immigration in the US.* Washington, DC: Pew Research Center.

Latino achievement in America. (2003, January 1). *The Education Trust.*

Legal issues for school districts related to the education of undocumented children. (2009). Washington, DC: National Education Association and National School Boards Association.

Living in America: Challenges facing new immigrants and refugees. (2006, August). Princeton, NJ: Robert Wood Johnson Foundation.

Lopez Castro, G. (2005, December). Sangre de mi Sangre: Menores migrantes en la migracion indocumentada. Presented at a conference at the University of Monterrey, Mexico.

Lopez, J. K. (2010). *Undocumented students and the policies of wasted potential.* El Paso, TX: LFB Scholarly Publishing.

Lopez, M. H., Gonzalez-Barrera, A., & Cuddington, D. (2013, June 19). Diverse origins: The nation's 14 largest Hispanic-origin groups. Washington, DC: Pew Research Center.

Lucas, Tamara. (1997). *Into, through, and beyond secondary school: Critical transitions for immigrant youth.* McHenry, IL: Delta Publishing.

Lukes, M. (2015). *Latino immigrant youth and interrupted schooling: Dropouts, dreamers, and alternative pathways to college.* Bristol, England: Multilingual Matters.

Macias, L. F. (2015, March 6). Addressing the impact of parental deportation on Latino/a students' post-secondary education goals. Presentation at Ohio Latino Education Summit. Akron, OH: University of Akron.

MacKinnon, H. (2014, July). *Education in emergencies: The case of the Dadaab refugee camps.* Centre for International Governance Innovation.

Mace-Matluck, B, Alexander-Kasparik, R., & Queen, R. (1998). *Through the golden door: Educational approaches for adolescent immigrants with limited schooling.* Washington, DC: Delta Publishing.

Manning, K. (2014, December 5). Dominican Republic revamps failing education system. *Deutsche Welle.*

Martinez, C. R., Jr., DeGarmo, D. S., & Eddy, J. M. (2004). Promoting academic success among Latino youths. *Latino Journal of Behavioral Sciences, 26,* 128–151.

Mead, A. (2003). *Year of no rain.* New York, NY: Farrar, Straus, and Giroux.

Medina, I. (2014, November). From violence to more violence in Central America. *Forced Migration Review,* pp. 74–75.

Menken, K. (2008). *English learners left behind: Standardized testing as language policy.* Clevedon, England: Multilingual Matters.

Mitchell, C. (2015, May 6). Undocumented students strive to adapt. *Education Week.*

Mitchell, C. (2015, July 8). Schools should see fewer unaccompanied minors this fall. *Education Week.*

Nazario, S. (2014). *Enrique's journey.* New York, NY: Ember Books.

Neuman, S., Copple, C., & Bredekamp, S. (2000). *Learning to read and write: Developmentally appropriate practices for young children.* Washington, DC: National Association for the Education of Young Children.

Noguera, P. A. (2014). Latino youth: Immigration, education, and the future. In A. Darder & R. D. Torres (Eds.), *Latinos and education: A critical reader.* New York, NY: Routledge.

North, D. (2009, September). The immigrant paradox: The stalled progress of recent immigrants' children. Washington, DC: Center for Immigrant Studies.

Nwosu, C., & Batalova, J. (2014, May 29). *Haitian immigrants in the United States.* Washington, DC: Migration Policy Institute.

Nwosu, C., & Batalova, J. (2014, June 18). *Immigrants from the Dominican Republic in the United States.* Washington, DC: Migration Policy Institute.

O'Loughlin, J. B. (2010). *Academic language accelerator.* New York, NY: Oxford University Press.

O'Loughlin, J. B. (2014). Picture books to help ELL access common core anchor reading standards. *Colorin Colorado.* http://www.colorincolorado.org/blog/picture-books-help-ells-access-common-core-anchor-reading-standards

O'Loughlin, J. B. (2012). Voices from the field: Teachers' reflection on coteaching experiences. In A. Hongisfeld & M. G. Dove (Eds.), *Coteaching and other collaborative practices in the EFL/ESL classroom: Rationale, research, reflections, and recommendations.* Charlotte, NC: Information Age Publishing.

O'Loughlin, J. B. (2013). Grade 3: What time is it? In M. Gottlieb & G. Ernst-Slavit (Eds.), *Academic language in diverse classrooms: Promoting content and language learning. Mathematics, Grades 3–5.* Thousand Oaks, CA: Corwin.

O'Loughlin, J. B. (2014). Beyond history: Glimpses into the past through picture books. In P. Spycher (Ed.), *Common core state standards in English language arts for English language learners: Grades K–5. Common core standards for English language learners,* Series Editor, Luciana C. deOliveira. Alexandria, VA: TESOL Press.

Orfield, G. (2002). Commentary. In M. Suárez-Orozco & M. Paez (Eds.), *Latinos: Remaking America* (pp. 389–397). Berkeley: University of California Press.

Page, B., & Maurizio, T. (forthcoming). "A Cycle of success: Extending learning for newcomers with high school volunteers." In M. Dantas-Whitney & S. Rilling (Eds.), *TESOL voices: Insider accounts of classroom life (Secondary learners' volume).* Alexandria, VA: TESOL Press.

Passel, J. (2011, Spring). Demography of immigrant youth: Past, present, and future. *Future of Children Journal, 21*(1), 18–42.

Patrick, H., & Mantzicopoulos, P. (2014). *Engaging young children with informational books.* Thousand Oaks, CA: Corwin.

Pennebaker, J. W. (1997). *Opening up: The healing power of expressing emotions* (2nd ed.). New York, NY: Guilford Press.

Pennebaker, J. W., & Smyth, J. M. (2016). *Opening up by writing it down: Improves health and eases emotional pain* (3rd ed.). New York, NY: Guilford Press.

Perez, W., Espinoza, R., Ramos, K., Coronado, H., & Cortes, R. (2009, May). Academic resilience among undocumented Latino students. *Hispanic Journal of Behavioral Sciences, 31*(2), 149–181.

Perry, K., & Hart, S. J. (2012, October). "We're kind of winging it": Preparing and supporting educators of refugee learners. *Journal of Adolescent & Adult Literacy, 56*(2), 110–122.

Refugee Education in 2002/2003. (2003, September). Geneva, Switzerland: United Nations High Commission on Refugees.

Refugee Resettlement Trends. (2015, June). New York, NY: United Nations High Commission on Refugees.

Refugees from Burma: Their backgrounds and refugee experience. (2007, June). Culture Profile No. 21. Washington, DC: Cultural Orientation Resource Center at the Center for Applied Linguistics.

Refugees from the Democratic Republic of the Congo. (2013). Washington, DC: Cultural Orientation Resource Center at the Center for Applied Linguistics.

Robertson, K., & Lafond, S. (n.d.). How to support ELL students with interrupted formal education (SIFEs). *Colorin Colorado*. Retrieved from http://www.colorincolorado.org/article/how-support-ell-students-interrupted-formal-education-sifes

Robson, B., & Lipson, J. (2002). *The Afghans: History and culture*. Washington, DC: Cultural Orientation Resource Center at the Center for Applied Linguistics.

Rodrigo, D. V., & Reitig, V. (2015, September). *Migrants deported from the United States and Mexico to the Northern Triangle: A statistic and socioeconomic profile*. Washington, DC: Migration Policy Institute.

Rong, X. L., & Preissle, J. (2009). *Educating immigrant students in the 21st century* (2nd ed.). Thousand Oaks, CA: Corwin.

Rossen, E., & Hull, R. (2013). *Supporting and educating traumatized students: A guide for school-based professionals*. New York, NY: Oxford University Press.

Roxas, K., & Roy, L. (2012). "That's how we roll": A Case study of a recently arrived refugee student in an urban high school. *Urban Review, 44*(4), 468–486.

Ruiz-de-Velasco, J., & Fix, M. (2000). *Overlooked and underserved: Immigrant students in US secondary schools*. Urban Institute: Washington, DC.

Rusen, S., Zong, J., & Batalova J. (2015, April 7). Cuban immigrants in the United States. Washington, DC: Migration Policy Institute.

Salinas, E. J. (2016, March). Eradicating learned pacifity: Preventing ELs from becoming long-term English learners. *Multilingual Educator*, 48–50.

Saragoza, A. M. (1989). *Mexican immigrant children in American schools: A brief sketch*. Berkeley, CA: California University Graduate School of Education.

Schifini, A. (1999, May). Reading instruction for older struggling readers. PREL Briefing Paper.

School Allocation Memorandum No. 81, FY 12. (2011, December 21). From Michael Tragale, Chief Financial Officer of New York City Schools to Community Superintendents, High School Superintendents, Children First Networks, and School Principals.

Served populations by state and country of origin. (2016, April 22). U.S. Department of Health and Human Services, Administration for Children and Families, Office for Refugee Resettlement.

Shattered lives: Challenges and priorities for Syrian children and women in Jordan. (2013). UNICEF Jordan Country Office.

Short, D., & Boyson, B. (2004). *Creating access: Language and academic programs for secondary school newcomers*. Center for Applied Linguistics: Washington, DC.

Short, D., & Boyson, B. (2012). *Helping newcomer students succeed in secondary school and beyond*. Washington, DC: Center for Applied Linguistics.

Short, D., & Echevarria, J. (2016). *Developing academic language with the SIOP model*. Boston, MA: Pearson Education.

Short, D., & Fitzsimmons, S. (2007). *Double the work: Challenges and solutions to acquiring language and academic literacy for adolescent English language learners—A report to Carnegie Corporation of New York*. Washington, DC: Alliance for Excellent Education.

SIFE: meeting the challenge [Video and PowerPoint on SIFE program]. (2013, Summer). New York City Department of Education. Retrieved from http://www.schools.nyc.gov

Souers, K., & Hall, P. (2016). *Fostering resilient learners: Strategies for creating a trauma-sensitive classroom.* Alexandria, VA: ASCD.

The state of education for Latino students. (2014, June). The Education Trust.

Stewart, M. A. (2015, September/October) "My journey of hope and peace:" Learning from adolescent refugees' lived experiences. *Journal of Adolescent and Adult Literacy, 59*(2), 149–150.

Suárez-Orozco, C., Baolian Qin, D., & Fruja Anthor, R. (2008). Adolescents from immigrant families. In Michael Sadowski (Ed.), *Adolescents at School* (2nd ed.). Cambridge, MA: Harvard Education Press.

Suárez-Orozco, C., Gaytán, F. X., Bang, H. J., Pakes, J., O'Connor, E., & Rhodes, J. (2010). Academic trajectories of newcomer immigrant youth. *Developmental Psychology, 46*, 602–618.

Suárez-Orozco, C., Rhodes, J., & Milburn, M. (2009). Unraveling the immigrant paradox: Academic engagement and disengagement among recently arrived immigrant youth. *Youth & Society, 41*, 151–185.

Suárez-Orozco, C., Suárez-Orozco, M., & Todorova, I. (2008). *Learning a new land: Immigrant students in American society.* Cambridge, MA: Belknap Press of Harvard University Press.

Supporting English language learners with limited prior schooling: A practical guide for Ontario educators in Grades 3–12. (2008). Ottawa, Ontario, Canada: Ontario Ministry of Education.

Temporary Protected Status. (2015, May 20). Department of Homeland Security official website. Retrieved from http://www.uscis.gov

Thomas, W., & Collier, V. (2002) *A national study of school effectiveness for language minority students' long term academic achievement.* Santa Cruz, CA: Center for Research in Education, Diversity, and Excellence.

Tovani, C. (2000). *I read it, but I don't get it: Comprehension strategies for adolescent readers.* Portland, ME: Stenhouse.

Tuchman, O. (2009). *Effective programs for English language learners (ELL) with interrupted formal education.* Indiana Department of Education.

Unaccompanied alien children U.S. law and policy backgrounder—Protecting the best interests of all children. (2014). Baltimore, MD: Lutheran Immigration and Refugee Service.

Unaccompanied children in schools: What you need to know. (2015). Colorin Colorado. Retrieved from http://www.colorincolorado.org/guide/unaccompanied-children-schools-what-you-need-know

Understanding and addressing the protection and immigrant children who come alone to the United States. (2013, February). Washington, DC: Kids in Need of Defense (KIND).

UNHCR Statistical Online Population Database. (2014). Geneva, Switzerland: United Nations High Commission on Refugees.

UNHCR Global Resettlement Statistical Report for 2013. (2014). Geneva, Switzerland: United Nations High Commission on Refugees.

Unite for Sight. (n.d.). Module 4 "Children and education in refugee camps" in Refugee Health Online Course. Retrieved from http://uniteforsight.org

Van Wyk, C. (2014). *Long walk to freedom: Illustrated children's edition*. London, UK: Macmillian Children's Books.

Walsh, C., & Prasker, H. (Eds.). (1991). *Literacy development for bilingual students: A manual for secondary teachers and administrators*. Boston: New England Multifunctional Resource Center for Language and Culture in Education at Massachusetts University.

Walqui, A. (2000). *Access and engagement: Program design and instructional approaches for immigrant students in secondary schools*. Center for Applied Linguistics: Washington, DC.

Wasen, R. E., & Morris, A. (2014, September 24). *Unaccompanied alien children: Demographics in brief*. Washington, DC: Congressional Research Services.

Wright, C., & Levitt, M. J. (2014). Parental absence, academic competence, and expectations in Latino immigrant youth. *Journal of Family Issues, 35*(13), 1754–1779.

Yousafzai, M. (2016). *I am Malala: How one girl stood up for education and changed the world*. New York, NY: Little Brown Books for Young Readers.

Zacarian, D. (2011). *Transforming schools for English learners: A comprehensive framework for school leaders*. Thousand Oaks, CA: Corwin.

Zacarian, D., & Haynes, J. (2012). *The essential guide for educating beginning English learners*. Thousand Oaks, CA: Corwin.

Zong, J., & Batalova. J. (2015, September 2). *Central American immigrants in the United States*. Washington, DC: Migration Policy Institute.

INDEX

A SAGE Publishing Company

Helping educators make the greatest impact

CORWIN HAS ONE MISSION: to enhance education through intentional professional learning.

We build long-term relationships with our authors, educators, clients, and associations who partner with us to develop and continuously improve the best evidence-based practices that establish and support lifelong learning.

Solutions you want. Experts you trust. Results you need.